I AM FARANG

I am Farang

Adventures of a
Peace Corps Volunteer in Thailand

Amy McGarry

ISBN: 978-0-578-45154-1

Book design by: Russel Davis, Gray Dog Press

Printed in the United States of America

For Mustapha and Sophia.

Contents

Preface

Farang (Thai: ฝรั่ง *[faràŋ], colloquially [falàŋ]) is a generic Thai word for someone of European ancestry, no matter where they may come from. The Royal Institute Dictionary 1999, the official dictionary of Thai words, defines the word as "a person of the white race".*
                                                                    —Wikipedia

I CHOSE THE TITLE *I am Farang* to be a constant reminder to the reader that the lens through which I looked while living in Thailand, was always that of a foreigner. It's a reminder that my perspective was always that of an American, with my American lens, filter, and perspective. As a foreigner, I was biased, and for this I apologize. My descriptions of Thai culture should always be read with that "grain of salt."

Also, I served in Peace Corps Thailand from 2003 to 2005. My experience was specific to that time in history. With time comes changes. For example, I was recently informed that the dog problem that you will read about in several different chapters, is no longer the problem it was back in the early 2000s.

I am Farang is also only one woman's experience as a Peace Corps volunteer. While some insights into the Peace Corps experience can be gleaned here, this book is not designed to be a primer on the Peace Corps. If you are a reader who is considering joining the Peace Corps, my advice is DO IT! That is, you should do it if you feel compelled, or called, or want to be a part of one of the greatest achievements of John

F. Kennedy. Yes, of course the hardships are real, and hard. But I would do it again in a second. In fact, I often think that maybe I will try to serve another term one day in the future.

If I come across as negative, it's mostly my attempts at humor and to be entertaining. I hope I have been at least a little bit successful.

Part One

Pre-Service Training

January, 2003 to March, 2003

Chapter 1

And So It Begins

NONE OF THIS SEEMED REAL TO ME until just this morning when I woke up in Thailand and went out to explore my new surroundings. I hit a nearby 7-11 only to discover I couldn't even buy a snack without major confusion. Never mind that EVERYONE was staring at me. I was the only white person in town, well, me and the 34 other PCVs (Peace Corps volunteers) staying in this town for our pre-service training. I hadn't slept much at all since boarding the airplane for Bangkok four days ago, so I was bordering on delirium, and desperate for coffee. Oh god, what have I gotten myself into…?

Always the early bird, of course I'm up at the crack of dawn before all the other PCVs. It's a source of pride that I will be the first one to explore this town in which we arrived late last night. As the sun brings light to the early morning market, I make my way to what appears to be a coffee stand. I may be an early bird, but lord help us all if coffee is not involved in the first minutes of the day.

I'm pleasantly surprised to find the weather is mild, pleasant, comfortable…especially early in the morning. Then again, it IS January, the middle of the "cold season" in Thailand. My guess is the temps are high 60s, low 70s. This is a huge relief to me, as when I was applying for a Peace Corps position, my one and only request was that I get sent to a country that was not too hot. I loathe hot weather. Never mind that almost all countries to which Peace Corps sends volunteers are in hot climates, I was begging for one of the former Soviet countries. One of the "stans," you know, Tajikistan, Kazakhstan, and weren't there several more countries ending in "stan?" More importantly, they weren't known to be excessively hot, right? My image of a "stan" citizen is definitely wearing a lot of clothes. Maybe fur.

But no. Despite my begging and pleading, I get assigned to Thailand. I cried when I got the news. Then I reminded myself, part of this adventure was the hardship and discomfort. I vowed then and there to embrace it. After all, don't people actually choose to vacation in Thailand? Must be some appeal.

I was doing a great job embracing the 70 degree morning at the market when I noticed that all the Thais were wearing jackets, just like my image of the Kazakhstanis! Maybe this is exactly where I was meant to be after all.

Five thirty a.m. and the market is already hopping. What are all these people doing out so early in the morning? It would later become clear that people come shopping early because: 1) they get first dibs on the freshest produce, fish and meat, 2) it's still nice and cool, and 3) they are buying for that morning's breakfast. Besides a quick trip to the closest Krispy Kreme Donuts to grab a baker's dozen of fresh glazed in the drive-thru, I never shopped for that morning's breakfast the morning of the breakfast. I don't know any Americans who do. Then again, I don't know of any markets in my town that sell live chickens to be butchered for that day's lunch, either.

Noticeably not wearing jackets is a long line of barefooted, shaved-headed, orange-robed monks, holding out bowls, begging for their daily food. Unlike the single, or sometimes paired beggars in my city who are dressed shabbily and usually have hair, (although sometimes not teeth), I like the symmetry of the orange robes and the bald heads. They almost look like clones. Oh crap. I've only been in this country four days and I'm already making racist comments about the locals. "Oh, you know, all Thai monks look the same." There's definitely a learning curve here.

It IS a coffee stand! My first adventure in Thai coffee culture! So exciting!!!

"I can do this!" I tell myself, to calm my nerves. Not only is everyone staring at me but I don't have any language training yet to get this coffee. Not to worry. I've watched plenty of Rick Steves on public television. Furthermore, it should be pretty darn obvious what I want, right? I smile at the lovely young coffee vendor and point to the brew. I hand her some coins. She hands me some coins back. More smiling. Easy peasy lemon squeezy!

But alas, I soon discover my morning coffee is a witch's brew of thick instant coffee, (instant!) and canned milk (canned!). Not to sound snobby, but I'm a coffee connoisseur. I have certain requirements of my coffee. It needs to be fresh ground. It needs to have half and half.

But I am sleep deprived and desperate. I remind myself that I am embracing the hardship, which just might mean sweet, instant coffee. I pull on my big girl panties and take a sip.

It's delicious.

And the price is right. At 25 cents a cup, she could give Starbucks a run for their money. She also keeps a stack of fried dough on the table and trusts you to tell her how many you ate. Tea is a weak jasmine brew, but free at the table. After I finish one cup of coffee, I order another, smiling at my first success as a Peace Corps volunteer.

I start class at 8:00 a.m. and go until 6:00 p.m. We're learning Thai language. We're learning about Thai culture, how to fit in and not to offend. We're learning a lot about staying safe and healthy.

We have an American doctor on staff, Dr. Jack, who reminds me of Woody Allen with a grey beard. His job is to educate us, inoculate us, and treat us, should we succumb to the ailments most common (or least) for Peace Corps volunteers in Thailand. Let's just say I had no idea diarrhea was such an exhaustive topic or that acne is one of the bigger threats to the Thailand volunteer community. And knee problems. We Westerners are unaccustomed to using squat toilets. Very hard on the knees. Who knew? Not to mention extensive time sitting on the floor criss-cross applesauce (formerly known as "Indian style"), toes never pointed toward another person, a major faux-pas in Thai culture.

Dr. Jack talks a lot about dengue fever. Dengue fever is a flu-like illness contracted through mosquitoes. We've heard so much hoopla about this dengue that the volunteers have started a dengue lottery. We've all contributed a sum of cash to the fund. First person to get dengue wins the pot! I actually hope it's me. Not just for the money, but because it seems like it would make a good story. And later I will come to discover that extended hospital stays in Bangkok are a luxury vacation to the Peace Corps volunteer in Thailand.

One of the best things about training is the young Thai people who are our language and culture experts and teachers. They speak English fluently and are ever-so patient with us. Every day we sit in groups of four volunteers and learn the most basic Thai. Survival Thai. How to order food. How to say the food is delicious. And how to tell our homestay "mother" that we are full. This will turn out to be the most useful information of all because Thai mothers are like the stereotypical Jewish mothers who will feed you until you explode if you are unable to convince them that you are indeed full.

The moments before meeting my homestay family were some of the scariest of my life and I almost passed out in my panic. But like most anxiety provoking experiences, the lead up to the event was much worse than the actual event. I knew ahead of time my host parents have a 20-year-old daughter who is away at college during the week but comes home on the weekends. There's also a 15-year-old son. I had also learned that two older "aunts" keep their traditional Thai style home immaculately clean. I'm told the mother of the household is quite "proper," whatever that means and compared to what?

When the families came to pick us up at the training site it was like being adopted. The PCVs are dressed in their finest volunteer-in-a-third-world-country attire, sitting in the front of the room, nervously glancing back to see if the families have arrived. Even though we've all been matched to our homestay families in advance, I get the urge to raise my hand and shout "Pick me! Pick me! Please pick me!"

Then all these Thai families start showing up, some with children, some with extended family members, all smiling from ear-to-ear. As our Thai teachers guided each family to their volunteer, the panic started choking me. Sweating, heart pounding, shaking. What was this about? I was a 34-year-old woman who had amassed years of experience including tragedy, travel and teaching teenagers. Still, I was terrified. How would we communicate? What if I didn't like the food? What if I made a faux pas? What if they don't like me and then think all Americans are awful and tell all their friends and then I've failed my whole mission of peace and friendship as a volunteer?

To my relief, I didn't pass out. And then there was no more time for anxiety. They were here! I was too busy trying to make a good impression to panic.

Smile? Check.

Bow with prayer hands? Check.

Nod and pretend I understand what's being said? Check.

Hallelujah! It soon became evident that my new host sister Nung spoke enough English, although flawed, to get some main points across. She told me we were going across the street to the market before heading back to the house.

She held my arm to escort me across the street like a little old lady, telling me, "Don't be nervous. Don't worry." She looked sweetly into my eyes. "Are you *tie-red*? Are you *tie-red*?" Yes, indeed I was very **tired**, so I nodded, smiling weakly, looking as pathetic as I could, to muster up sympathy from my sister. So concerned was Nung with my nerves, my worry, my fatigue, I'm pretty sure she would have carried me across the street and through the market, were she able. Instead, she kept a gentle hold on my arm, and while as a rule, I am not one who likes to be touched, especially by someone I've just met, I found Nung's gentle grip and tender caress of my arm so comforting, so soothing, I welcomed it.

I knew that my host father was an insurance salesman and is away from home most of the month, but he was here for the adoption event and had the brand new company car to take me home in. Wait, what? A brand new company car? Aren't I supposed to be clinging tightly to the roof of some decrepit dusty bus? Or at least sharing my seat with some live chickens? Yet there I found myself, getting into a brand new, immaculate, luxury sedan with leather seats and air conditioning. Somehow that didn't seem quite right. But who was I to complain?

Chapter 2

Is This Cheating?

"I think this whole experience is about growth and self-knowledge. Perhaps I have capacities I never knew I had."
Jan. 10, 2003, Journal entry.

UPON ARRIVAL AT WHAT WOULD BE my new home for the next two months of my pre-service training, I find a gorgeous traditional Thai-style house full of shining teak wood flooring and cabinets filled with antiques and ceramics. Not at all the corrugated tin-roofed shanty I had expected as a Peace Corps volunteer in a Third World country. The house stands high on columns, an age-old Thai precaution against flooding. The elegant house connects to a much more rustic house by an open-air wooden walkway.

The first thing I must do upon entering the house is stop at the shrine to Buddha, get on my knees and bow three times placing my head to the floor. Then Nung shows me to my bedroom, which is actually her room. While many Thais sleep on mats on the floor, I see Nung's room has a bona fide bed. Instead of a twin mattress however, it's topped with a plastic, one-inch thick plastic pad. Okay, maybe this is how Thai people prefer to sleep? Maybe mattresses are too expensive? Maybe mold or mildew is an issue because of the humidity? No, I'm pretty sure they have mattresses in Florida so the humidity can't be the issue. Screens on the windows mean I won't even need the Peace Corps issued mosquito net.

Then, my biggest question about the house is finally addressed. When Nung shows me the bathroom I heave a sigh of relief to see, not a hole in the ground over which I'd be forced to squat, but a genuine sit-your-bottom-on-a-seat Western-style toilet. And can it be? Yes! Toilet paper! Is this cheating? Nung points to a plastic box on the wall attached to the shower and says, "Hot water." What?!? A hot water shower? This is definitely cheating!

And yet, looking for a sink, I see none. Instead, I see huge white porcelain tiled vats filled with water. Plastic bowls sit next to the vats. Plastic bowls will grow to be my friends throughout my whole Thai experience as, once filled with water from the vats, serve to rinse my face, wash down my toothpaste that I spit on the floor, and in the absence of the toilet paper, rinse off my bottom.

Before our host families adopted us, our cultural training included the nitty-gritty, down-and-dirty, nuts-and-bolts of everyday life. Of course, we had all researched Thai life before we came. I knew traditionally, Thais, like most of the people in the world, use what we call so poetically and picturesquely, "the squat toilet." But this research took place back in the old school days, around the turn of the century, 2003 to be exact, and one couldn't simply "google" for information back then. Google wasn't even a verb back then. We read books. I don't remember ever seeing an actual picture of a squat toilet in my books for research. What did it look like? How did it actually work? The mere concept of a squat toilet was a source of pride for all of us volunteers. The very proof of the hardship of our two-year-service that we eagerly embraced.

OK. That's a lie. Some of the other volunteers were super excited about using a squat toilet. I was not. Nevertheless, we all had to be trained on how to actually use the damn things. Potty training 2.0? Toilet training for adults? Whatever you want to call it, I was expecting an informational handout, with diagrams perhaps. Maybe some advice from our trainers. Instead, my mouth dropped open as I watched a young Thai man, one of our trainers, demonstrating in a role play, a real life drama, how to take a shit on a squat toilet. I was so busy giggling and nudging the volunteer next to me and sharing wide eyed, astonished looks that I missed the relevant details of the training! Plus, as he was fully clothed, we couldn't get the full effect anyway. Looks like my potty-on-the-squatty training would be by trial and error. And were there ever errors!

After that day I had more than my fair share of experience with squat toilets. And I still have questions and concerns about using them. For one, our demonstrator should have been female and she should have role played taking a piss as well as taking a shit. When a woman squats over a hole in the ground, the stream of urine does not move in a straight line down into the hole. It shoots out at an angle. Hundreds of times I've peed over a hole, maybe thousands, considering all the nights out drinking and how many times I needed to pee as the beer went through me. I can count on one hand how many times all of the urine actually went into the hole. I've tried facing different directions. I've tried standing up, which is actually one of the more effective stances. But there's still the splash factor.

Speaking of splash...the traditional Thai method of wiping oneself doesn't involve toilet paper. Instead, historically one kept a bucket of water next to the squatty, which also had a faucet to refill the bucket. Floating in the bucket is my friend the plastic bowl. One scoops up water from the bucket into the plastic bowl and splashes oneself off using one's hand. Very refreshing. Very clean. Modern technology such as it is, however, means that often a toilet stall will include an actual hose to spray oneself, in lieu of using one's hand to splash. It's brilliant, really. Picture the hose you pull out of the kitchen sink when you're washing dishes. Even more clean and refreshing, and one of the many aspects of Thai life I grow to appreciate and love. The real luxury for me as a Westerner however, is the doubly-whammy of the hose AND toilet paper, which can very rarely be found. Rinse. Dry. Repeat.

After his Academy Award performance in the toilet training category, our Thai actor continues to act out the daily rituals. Next is bathing. Thais value bodily cleanliness and are a very clean people so bathing multiple times a day is encouraged. Especially since they think Westerners are dirty and smell like cheese. And because in Thailand we sweat. All. Day. Long. Thai people are mortified that some Westerners don't even bathe twice a day, even when we explain that where we live we don't sweat all day, every day, even in the winter, aka "cold season."

Traditionally Thais bathe via "splash bath," which our trainer so kindly models. Back to the friendly plastic bowls of water and those big vats of water in my host family's bathroom. If you've ever bathed a toddler and rinsed the shampoo out of the little one's hair by pouring water from a container over their head, you've got the concept of a splash bath. Only you do it standing up. In the middle of the bathroom floor. With cold water from a huge vat, or smaller bucket, depending. Doesn't that make a mess on the bathroom floor? Yes and no. Thai bathrooms brilliantly have drains in the middle of the floor that are built to slant slightly towards the drain.

This is why I'm surprised to find a "shower" in my host family's bathroom. Not a shower stall, mind you, but a shower head and a plastic box for heating water attached to the bathroom wall. I could still shower in the middle of the bathroom floor, if I chose to. What I discover instead is that after riding my bicycle home from training in 90-100 degree heat, the last thing I want is a hot shower. That vat of water has been sitting all day at room temperature and is a lovely cool temperature, like diving into a swimming pool on a hot day. Furthermore, the water pressure from the shower is dismal compared to a nice full bowl of water poured over one's body. The splash bath is heavenly. Except on cool winter mornings, when I fake it, and take more of a "spit bath" than a "splash bath."

When Nung guides me across the walkway to the attached rustic house, I see that this is where food is prepared and where I will make my way every morning to eat breakfast by myself at a table with chairs. The table and chairs are noteworthy because Thai meals are traditionally eaten sitting on the floor. Unlike my solitary breakfasts, family dinners are served on the floor in the living room. Hence, I will grow to understand the knee problems associated with volunteering in Thailand. However, sitting criss-cross on the floor at dinner is actually much harder on my hips than on my knees. Either knees or hips, it's never comfortable.

My host family invites my training group, the three other volunteers in my neighborhood, to dinner that first night. I'm so relieved.

Four volunteers make up each training group. Each training group lives in the same village where we have our language and culture training together and start practicing teaching in the village school. My group, or "village people" includes Sarah, a quiet woman my age from Minnesota, and two young bucks fresh out of college, Dan and Mark. Mark is housed right next door to me in an equally lavish setting. Sarah's host family is of much more modest means. Dan's is somewhere in the middle.

We all gather cross-legged around a foot-high table as the mother and aunties bring dish after dish to the table. My host father tries to impress us with the little English he has, by pointing to the appetizer on the table, "Pig. Pig." And this is why some people become vegetarian. I never thought about how we call the meat of the animal that we eat something different from the name of the animal. Now all I can do is picture little Wilbur from *Charlotte's Web*. Even though I've lost my appetite, I'm desperate to please my host family so I dig into the pig and exclaim "*Aroi!*" It means "delicious" and it's one of the only Thai words I know how to say.

Smiling and nodding. Nodding and smiling. I feel like I'm in a sit-com. Surely a Seinfeld episode parodied this scenario. It's awkward and exhausting. Bedtime can't come early enough.

In training we were warned that Thai people have a different sense of privacy than Americans. They think nothing of looking through our suitcases and other stuff when we're not home. Not to worry, we're told, they're just curious.

At night I dream of aliens approaching me as I sleep, peering into my face, checking me out, poking, prodding, scrutinizing me. Their faces, coincidentally, resemble one of my host aunties. It's terrifying and so real that upon waking I half believe it really happened. The dreaming is the only way I know I have slept. I'm so uncomfortable on my one inch thick mat I could swear I haven't slept at all.

Chapter 3

So Many Mysteries

IN THE MORNING I make my way across the bridge to the rustic house to have my breakfast. Walking by the parents' room, its door open, I nonchalantly glance in, and notice a mattress on the floor. An authentic, Western-style, twin mattress, that coincidentally looks like it fits perfectly into the bed in my bedroom. At least Nung still gets to sleep in comfort the two whole days of the week she's actually sleeping at the house. Whereas I will embrace the discomfort, I remind myself with chagrin, massaging my stiff and aching back.

In retrospect, having grown to understand Thai hospitality, I have no doubt that my comfort was of utmost importance to my host family. My guess is Peace Corps instructed them to give me the pre-school mattress. They might even assume that is what I prefer, one of their own mysteries about Americans, or maybe they just tell themselves that.

As soon as I sit down, my host mother goes to the cupboard behind me and removes the many offerings that she sets before me. She says nothing to me. I say nothing but "*khop khun ka,*" or "thank you," to her. More smiling, more nodding.

I try not to think about how this food has been stored overnight uncovered in a cupboard. I'm okay with it until I see the same dish reappear for the third time. Then I get a little grossed out. One of the many mysteries in my life as a volunteer is, why do leftovers get stored in a cupboard and not the refrigerator, when the family does indeed own a refrigerator? I pretend they actually do put the food in the refrigerator overnight, then take it out and put in the cupboard before serving it the next morning. I tell myself that all those times I've left the uneaten pizza out on the counter overnight then ate it straight from the box (breakfast of champions!) has trained my system for just this experience. I haven't gotten sick yet. In fact, the only discomfort so far is the very swollen and painful immunization site on my arm for typhoid/dyptheria, my 6th round of shots since arriving in country.

My host mother monitors closely what I choose to eat from the array of selections placed before me. She's determining my preferences, as I will come to see in the future that the offerings start to become more limited to only the items I've chosen previously. There's really no such thing as "breakfast food" as opposed to food for other meals. Hot dogs appear to be a favorite. Or maybe they think that's what I prefer. Isn't there a song with the line, "What's more American than hot dogs?..." Or maybe they know Americans eat sausage for breakfast and hot dogs are close enough. Another mystery.

After breakfast, I wash my dishes as I've been instructed. I squat down onto the stoop outside the kitchen and scoop up some water into a bin. I scrape excess food into a container, wash the dishes in *cold* water with a little soap, then pour the excess water through a crack in the stoop. It's like camping in a tree house. Yet another mystery, is, in a house with the modern conveniences of a toilet, shower and a refrigerator, there is no running water or sink. Then again, why would they need running water or a sink? To help with laundry, for one reason.

Oh, lordy, laundry. The bane of my existence as a volunteer in a Third World country. I am no stranger to old-style clothes washing. When I was a child the washing machine in my house was so old it didn't have a spin cycle. It was just a big open-top bin with an agitator to wash the clothes. After rinsing, you had to feed the soaking wet clothes into a wringer which was two rollers that turned automatically (high tech!) and so tightly squeezed the fabric that every drop of water was wrung out.

It was great fun as a child to feed the wet clothes through the wringer. But it was a fine line you had to learn between getting close enough for the rollers to suck in the fabric and getting so close that your fingers got pinched between the rollers. Ouch.

Alas, here there are no rollers, no wringer. Just the clothes washer's bare hands. I'm not a weak person but why, oh why can I never squeeze enough water from the clothes? When I hang my clothes on the line, they aren't dripping, but pouring excess water. I desperately miss the automatic wringer and the whole damn experience makes me feel like I've been through the proverbial wringer.

The mystery is, while my host family splurged on the refrigerator, why wouldn't they buy an automatic washing machine? Probably because they have the aunties to do the laundry.

So it's the aunties who teach me how to wash my own clothes, as the Peace Corps staff has instructed them. Clearly, given their druthers, they'd just wash the clothes themselves. That would be much easier than trying to teach the pathetic farang how to do it herself. Remember the aunties don't speak a word of English and my Thai is still limited to "delicious!" which doesn't get me far in the laundry circuit.

Through gestures, it appears they want me to wash my clothes in the bathroom. This makes no sense to me. I've seen how laundry is done in Thailand. Most houses have big wash bins outside near the clothesline. The bathroom has no big wash bins. I can only assume this was for my privacy. Although everyone else in Thailand washes their underwear out in the open, I am special. In a society where everyone has their place in the hierarchy, it turns out, as an American in her 30s, with a degree or two under my belt, I'm actually held in pretty high esteem. Therefore, God forbid anyone sees MY undies.

Alone in the bathroom with the door closed I go through the motions of throwing some water and detergent onto my dirty clothes, right on the floor. I kind of slosh them around together, pour some more water over them to rinse off the soap. I come out a few minutes later, holding my dripping clothes in my hands, smiling and nodding.

The aunties, however, are not smiling and nodding. In fact, their brows are furrowed, they're shaking their heads and tsk-tsking. I don't need to understand Thai to know they are disappointed.

Apparently they are giving up on the bathroom washing idea all together as they grab my wet clothes and motion for me to follow them down the stairs outside to their clothes washing station. Still clucking and tsking…

Now I'm introduced to the age old process of women washing clothes by hand. They demonstrate the method. One big bin gets detergent, which must be swirled and sloshed by hand to promote lather. Two big bins for water only, for two steps in the rinsing process. While no words are needed to see what to do in this learn-by-watching, learn-by-doing process, they talk away in Thai, and I nod and smile my understanding. They show how to rub the clothes together for washing. I try to imitate what each hand does, but I never get it quite right. They always take it from me and finish the washing. The rinsing is easier. And I start to relax and breathe into the experience, the sound of splashing water, the wet coolness on my skin. If one is mindful, this is meditative.

Clothes have a hierarchy here, too. The nicer work clothes, like dresses, must be washed first, then more casual clothes, lastly undergarments. There's something quite intimate about a woman you don't know, who doesn't speak your English, demonstrating the art of washing the arm pits of your shirts, the crotch of your panties. They model adding a little extra dry detergent, scrubbing hard. Here we bond. Here we connected. We may not speak the same language. We may not understand each other's culture. But we know the experience of being a woman.

My undies are clean and hanging out for the whole world to see. They've instructed me to hang them on the lowest line, where they belong. I understand this. What I don't understand is how to wring my clothes free of water by hand before hanging them to dry. That is still a mystery to me.

Chapter 4

Not Crazy, Drunk

TRAINING FOR THE ACTUAL WORK of being an education volunteer entails a kind of "student teaching" at a school in our village. Every day after breakfast I ride my bicycle to the village school where I teach some English, train some teachers, and have my own language and culture lessons. What a relief to learn that the school where I'll be working for eight weeks has only a squat toilet. With no toilet paper, only the vat of water. Thank goodness I am not cheating after all!

Because I'm a trained and experienced teacher with a TESL (Teaching English as a Second Language) certificate, I excel at the student-teaching part of my training. My own language learning is another story. Prior to arrival in country, I took it upon myself to learn some Thai language. I bought the books, the CDs, the dictionaries, and made flash cards. I devoted hours to studying. And by the time I left for Thailand, I had a working vocabulary of about five words. I wasn't worried. Surely immersion would be the key to my language success. I was to be greatly disappointed.

Language class proves to be frustrating, humbling, and humiliating. Nothing sticks. My Thai teacher asks us questions in Thai. The other students seem to understand the question, but all I hear is gobbledygook. Like many teachers, I am also the worst discipline problem. I refuse to follow the "Thai language only" rule during class. Our language teacher is so kind and gentle he doesn't have the heart to enforce the rule. Or maybe he is just afraid of me, the big, loud farang lady. The irony? My future will find me making my living as an English language teacher where I have to enforce the "English only" rule in class.

While it seems I'm not learning any Thai language, slowly but surely I can remember a few words. Each night in my homestay home, the whole family watches Thai soap operas on TV. Excited that I can finally contribute to the family discussion more than a smile and a nod, I point to the crazy-acting woman on TV and proudly exclaim, "*ba ba bo bo*!"

I can remember the word for crazy, because it's so fun to say. *Ba ba bo bo. Ba ba bo bo.* In training, we play a game to see who can say it fastest. However, apparently I had misdiagnosed the madwoman in the soap opera. The old "auntie" with the rotten teeth and bad breath corrects me, "*Mao*!" *Mao* is another word I have committed to memory. It means "drunk." Not the verb in the sense of having had something to drink. I have no idea what that word is in Thai, but as in plastered, wrecked, hammered, loaded, or down right shit-faced from too much Thai whiskey or *bia* (beer). There's a reason Peace Corps volunteers learn that word so early in their tenure. And little did I know that that little word would become emblematic to my Peace Corps experience.

At the risk of stereotyping, Thais like to party. So do college students. Which is what most of my cohort of Peace Corps volunteers basically is, as many of them have recently graduated. Oh, the early 20s, that age when many of us indulge, experiment, go overboard…make mistakes. Put the party-lovin' Thais and their acute sense of hospitality together with a bunch of college grads…what do you get? A recipe for a whole lot of *ba ba bo bo mao!*

Like many societies, alcohol is tied intimately to social invents in Thailand. Beer or whiskey flows freely at all events and "events" happen frequently. Weekly. Daily. Sometimes a wedding. Sometimes a holiday. Sometimes a welcome party for a foreign volunteer. Furthermore, the booze in Thailand is cheap and it's strong. In fact, alcoholism is rampant in Thailand, mostly among men. Although, when the whiskey is flowing at an event and the dancing starts up, it's not uncommon to see the little old ladies off their rockers[1] going wild in a drunken combination of traditional Thai dance and twerking.

This happened at an event I attended which was actually a "monk-becoming" ceremony, the celebration of two brothers becoming monks. Everyone got sloppy drunk and danced around while the poor monks-becoming sat there in lotus position, unable to partake in the drink and dance. During the ceremony, one of the monks kept screwing up the chant, or mantra, and would start to giggle and have to be corrected by the also giggling monk leader. This was hilarious to the drunken audience.

In training we are warned about the temptation of libations. A psychologist is invited in for a special training session. She explains that living in a foreign culture is stressful and it's not a good idea to use alcohol as a coping mechanism. But the power of suggestion is too strong. That night a bunch of us get together and, realizing how stressed we are, decide drinking is just what the Doctor ordered. We conveniently forget the part about its hazards. When in Rome, and all, so we bust out with the karaoke, a Thai standard in merry-making. Note to self: Next time I sing karaoke with a bunch of 20-somethings, choose something a little more modern than Donna Summer's "Hot Stuff." It's more fun if the audience knows of the song.

Yep, when it comes to stress management or "culture shock," Thai whiskey is good medicine.

---

1 Actually Thailand has no rockers. Little old lady ladies don't even sit. They squat. They circle up in squat position chewing betel nut, which gets them high, and turns their teeth red. It's something Thai women look forward to as the get close to old age.

Chapter 5

Culture Shock: The Angry Phase

THE TERM CULTURE SHOCK refers to the 2nd phase of the four "Stages of Adjustment" that most people go through when living in a foreign country. The first phase is the honeymoon phase, which is exactly what it sounds like. Everything is new, exciting, fun, wonderful! You are so in love with your new home. It's the reason so many people love travel. Short-term travel is all about the honeymoon phase. I left the honeymoon phase and hit culture shock my fourth week in Thailand. It affects each person differently, but typical reactions can include homesickness, depression, and anger. I was angry. Angry at everything. Angry at the hot weather, angry about foods I didn't like, angry at the sound of the Thai language, and angry that everyone asked me what I had eaten every day.

In fact, almost everything about living in Thailand at this time infuriated me. My anger starts at 4:00 in the morning when the damn neighborhood roosters start their cock-a-doodle-dooin'. I toss and turn for a couple of hours, cursing them, and chickens in general, until the sun comes up, at which time, the roosters have stopped. However, at this time hundreds of varieties of birds have started their lovely and not so lovely songs so loud and with such a cacophony of noise that I'm sure I live in an aviary.

My morning symphony would also not be complete without the barking dogs. Dogs run wild in Thailand, literally. As a Buddhist culture, Thais don't believe in euthanizing animals. They also don't seem to believe in sterilization. Most of these dogs don't have homes. They suffer from all sorts of diseases, including rabies, and especially mange. I knew the word "mangy" in my life in America. But I don't think I ever knew there was such a real thing as "the mange" until I saw these dogs in the streets. Instead of fur, they are covered with scabs in different stages of healing. They are mean and scary, too, growling and snarling. Sometimes they chase us on our bikes. Thai people won't euthanize homeless, mangy, rabid dogs, but they treat them like shit, which is one of the contradictions that's infuriating and is contributing to my culture shock. Of course those dogs are mean to people when it's people who kick them and throw rocks at them. Since they belong to no one and pounds don't exist, let alone any form of Humane Society, they are left to scrounge for food. They are always hungry.

We ask our Thai trainers how Thai people can be so cruel to the dogs. "They are considered dangerous," we are told. It's confusing. Confusion is another symptom of culture shock.

But in the early morning when I'm trying to sleep, I almost understand the cruelty to dogs. My anger gets to the point where I could actually throw something at the dogs who are barking constantly. Plus crowing roosters. Plus singing birds. It all equals no sleep for me. The good news is that my bed is so hard and my pillow so big I probably couldn't sleep even if it were dead quiet.

Not only am I sleep deprived, but I've developed a stomach condition that keeps me mildly nauseous at all times. My host mother, bless her heart, offers me new foods for breakfast every morning. Who knew there were so many breakfast foods? Eggs, of course. Rice, not so surprising. Hot dogs. Salad. Fish ball soup. During the honeymoon phase, I gladly tried everything. Of course there were things I didn't care for, but that was part of the adventure. It's like the honeymoon phase of your marriage. Sure some things about your spouse are mildly annoying, but during this phase, it's all part of the adventure and you can tolerate almost anything!

Yes, I was adventurous with my palette. I tried the squid, which I don't even like back home, so not surprisingly I didn't care for here, either. I tried countless versions of fish, usually with the head on and eyeball staring right at you. These fish were almost always delicious, surprisingly, because I am not much of a fan of fish back home. I even tried the fish brain. It wasn't really a dare, but I was definitely trying to prove myself worthy of the other young volunteers, all adventurous to the nth degree. So, at a restaurant with a group of volunteers, when one asks, "Are you going to eat the brains? If you're not, I'd really like them[2]," I respond with false bravado that of course I'm going to eat the brains, but I'd be happy to share them. In fact, they were delicious, but it was kind of gross getting to them as you had to crack open the skull.

So that saying "the honeymoon is over" hits hard relative to food. I'm feeling much less adventurous with my eating. The consistent, persistent nausea doesn't help. Even foods I like start to make me gag, literally. And during culture shock, while we miss many things from home, mostly we miss familiar and favorite foods. I've started to miss familiar foods terribly. I would give my left arm for some pizza, nachos, or just chips and salsa. I'd give my right arm for a sandwich. My firstborn for a cheeseburger and fries.

Culture shock also means becoming annoyed with the most innocent customs. For example, Thais always ask, "What did you eat?" It's as common as "How are you?" It's almost like "What's up?" in the U.S. So when I'm riding my bike back home from training and strangers call out to me, "What did you eat?" I wish I had thought to answer, "A cheeseburger!" That would have blown their minds. But no. I say, "Fried

---

2 I'm starting a list of things I never thought I'd hear. First on the list: "Are you going to eat the brains? If you're not, I'd really like them."

rice," because I know how to say that. What I really want to say is "None of your goddamn business!" And "Why do you give a shit what I've eaten anyway?" That's culture shock.

During the honeymoon phase, this inquiry "What did you eat? What did you eat?" was cute and funny, almost endearing. Now it's just plain weird and annoying. If you stop and talk to them, the next thing they are going to say is guaranteed.

"It's hot today, right?" they'll say, fanning themselves, looking flustered from the heat. But still smiling, always smiling, the smile for which Thais are famous.

I want to scream, "Yes, it's hot! Of course it's hot! This is a tropical country! It's hot every fucking day! And aren't you fucking used to it by now???" But no. I smile. Because I am in "The Land of Smiles," an ambassador for peace and goodwill. Sighing inwardly I nod and reply, "Yes, it's very hot today."

In training, our Thai counterparts explain this line of questioning to us. They say it is just Thai culture. Thais like to keep things on the surface, instead of getting into the deeper, darker realities of how we are doing, which is suffering like mad from culture shock and mad as hell at everyone because of it. So they talk about food. They talk about the weather. They are masters of small talk. Which I desperately need to practice. For in the midst of my culture shock, the weekend comes, and I have a full day with my host family, alone, with no other volunteers. My host sister is not home from college this weekend, so there is not a lick of English spoken. This is supposed to be very good for me. This is the immersion, where I'm forced to practice the limited Thai language I've learned, and hopefully learn even more. Instead, I smile a lot. I nod a lot. I eat the dried bananas and assure my host family that I like the dried bananas. I asked "What's this?" over and over and over, simply to make conversation. Did I remember any of the answers? No. By the end of the day, I'm so frustrated and I exhausted I begin to wonder if I'll make it through this training period, let alone two years.

The funny thing about culture shock is that even though you know the reason you feel so annoyed, so irritated, so angry, it doesn't help one stinkin' bit to know why you feel this way. What does help to know is that it will pass. There's no way to predict when, or how often it will return, but this, too, shall pass.

Chapter 6

How to Earn Good Karma and Appease Mischievous Spirits

MY HOST MOTHER IS A DEVOUT BUDDHIST. First thing every morning she lights incense and prays on her hands and knees to the Buddhist shrine inside the house. The shrine includes statues and pictures of Buddha and various VIP monks. After lighting the incense and candles, she sets down small offerings of food and water. She often offers fresh flowers as well. The shrine is large, taking up half the wall in the living room, right between my bedroom and the bathroom. This is quite awkward for me. It seems utterly disrespectful to pass this woman praying on her knees and go into the bathroom and pee. What if I accidentally passed gas really loudly while she was praying? As uncomfortable as it gets, I wait until she's done praying.

After praying to Buddha, she goes outside with offerings of food and drink to place in the spirit house in the front yard. A spirit house is a miniature Thai style house, raised up on a pillar like traditional Thai houses so that the house itself is about eye-level. They remind me of very ornate bird houses. You see them everywhere in Thailand, of varying sizes and elegance. Thai people place them in their yards or in front of businesses to house the spirits that may be up to mischief otherwise. Not only do the Thais provide shelter for these unpredictable spirits, but in order to bribe them into submission, the spirits are provided food and drink. Apparently, if the spirits are happy they won't curse, haunt, or bring bad luck to the residents on the property.

Praying to Spirit House.

It's always interesting to look inside different houses and see what treats the spirits have been given. While the types of food varied, one commonality was the drink. It was always Strawberry Fanta. At first I just assumed that spirits were especially fond of Strawberry Fanta. Fanta is very popular among the living in Thailand. Especially orange. Maybe strawberry was an acquired taste specific to the spirit world?

Much later I would learn that red Fanta symbolizes the blood that used to be part of animal sacrifice. I never look at Strawberry Fanta the same way.

My host mother lights incense and prays at the spirit house. Observing, I'm mesmerized.

I begin to feel ghosts everywhere and wonder if the Thai reverence for ghosts actually encourages their active presence. My dreams at night are so real, I become convinced the ghosts are toying with me. As a general rule, I do not scare easily. I'm not afraid of ghosts. I used to wish I could encounter a ghost. But I awake from the dreams quite frightened. I don't trust the ghosts of my dreams. Maybe I should be the one providing the libations to the spirit house.

Although the Buddhist religion doesn't provide regular services like Christianity, Judaism and Islam do, one can go to the local temple, called a *wat* in Thai, at any time, and pray. The prayer ritual includes bowing your forehead to the floor three times while on your knees. Then you pray for compassion or wisdom or good things to come to your enemy. Other rituals inside the temple include lighting incense and candles, banging a gong, sticking pressed gold paper onto the Buddha statue, and shaking fortune sticks to have your fortune told. I shook the sticks for my fortune and was assured that any hardship I will have will be short lived. Phew! That's good to know. I went through these rituals at three different wats in one day.

While the devout Buddhist can perform these rituals at any time, there are also the Buddhist festival days, like holidays, that seem to come almost every week. In addition, one can request for a monk to hold a prayer session at any time. This requires only that you bring a gift basket to the monk. I participated in one such ceremony and was reminded of the Catholic church services from my childhood, what with offering to the monks and the praying/chanting repeated by the attendees and the sprinkling of the water. I actually enjoyed the experience, even though the chants (in Sanskrit) were too long for me to repeat accurately and it's quite painful to sit for such a long time in the required position of half-kneeling/half-sitting.

Buddhism is inherent in Thai culture, and there is no separation of church and state. Every morning at school the whole student body gathers on the lawn and after singing the national anthem, faces the wat and recites a prayer/chant led by one of the students.

Usually when my host mother or host aunties speak to me in Thai, I'm sure they're saying "What the hell are you doing, dumbass American?" or "Lazy American! Get your ass out of bed and do something!" But they are awfully friendly and smiley about it, so it's okay. On this particular day, however, I managed to understand through words, okay, mostly through pointing and other sign language, that I've been invited to feed the monks. Does that conjure images of baby monks in high chairs being spoon fed from jars of Gerber fruit?

Feeding monks rice.

No, no. Actually, I've been invited to garner some good karma by participating in the morning ritual of giving food to the monks. This is one way Buddhists earn their good karma. It's my understanding that Buddhist monks can only consume food that is given to them. Therefore, every morning at the crack of the dawn, with their alms bowls in hand, they walk through the village, single file, robed in saffron orange robes, barefoot and bald-headed as always. Villagers come out with big bowls of food, usually rice, so the monks will have sustenance for the day. Many times I've witnessed my host mother in this ritual.

Because Buddhist customs and rituals are so prevalent in Thai society, our training for volunteer service includes extensive guidelines for etiquette and respectful behavior when involved in these customs or rituals. I know one NEVER touches a monk. When it came time for me to give food to the monks, I was so worried about showing the appropriate respect and not accidentally touching the monk, I ended up bowing and kneeling, my face reddening in embarrassment as the monks laughed at me. One thing about those monks; they sure are a happy lot. I scoop rice into their bowl, bask in their warm smiles, relish in the good karma I've earned for the day.

This day is also laundry day. I gather up my soiled clothes and carry them down into the early morning coolness of the patio. I've grown to enjoy the hand-washing of my clothes. Crouching down with the buckets of fresh-smelling water in the cool morning surrounded by lush greenery and colorful flowers, the rhythmic, splashing up and down, is meditative. I lose all sense of time. I feel connected to a feminine ritual spanning the ages. I think I've gotten the hang of it now, but after I have hung all my clothes on the line, Auntie #1 has taken each piece and rehung it. I don't mind. I smile and nod my appreciation.

Chapter 7

Adventures in Bicycling, Boogers, and Bravery

THE BICYCLE IS QUINTESSENTIAL to every Peace Corps volunteer's experience. We are not allowed to drive. We can't rely on our host families to chauffeur us. Public transportation is not guaranteed for where we need to go. The solution is the good old fashioned bicycle. Of course, we are required to wear helmets. Riding in groups in our business-casual attire (we are required to dress professionally, as dictated by our social standing, per Thai standards of social conduct). If we were in the U.S. we'd be mistaken for Mormon missionaries. But in Thailand, where anyone of social standing high enough to dress in business attire is NOT riding a bicycle, and where no one, not even on a motorcycle, wears a helmet, let alone on a bicycle, we just look ridiculous. And the Thai people we pass on the street daily let us know by pointing and laughing. "*Farang!*" "*Farang!*"

Yes, we know we are foreigners. We will forever be baffled by the Thai need to point this out to us, over and over and over. We will continue to be shocked at how they don't think it's impolite. But manners are very culturally specific. Even though we know it's ethnocentric and unfair to judge a people for their "bad manners," we are human, so we complain about how rude our host countrymen are. We also forget that our own behavior is riddled with oddities to our host culture, many which seem impolite or downright rude to them. All the training in the world can't prevent us from breaking rules of etiquette.

I was once reprimanded by a Thai colleague for yawning without covering my mouth. Like an ashamed, chastised child, trying to save face with a tit for tat, I pointed out that in MY country it's rude to pick your nose in public, or at least when others can see.

"Really?" The Thai colleague was shocked.

"Oh yes," I proclaimed, vindicated. "Americans think it's disgusting."

I told myself I was providing a lesson in American culture, but really I was getting my digs in for having been called out on my own impropriety.

While there's no shame in mining for gold up one's nostril mid-conversation with another person, the mouth, however, is off limits. Well, not off limits. After meals it's common for people to clean their teeth with a toothpick, but they will always cover their mouth with the other hand while doing so. I try to remember to cover my mouth from now on should I be unable to suppress a yawn in public. I wonder if I will get to the point where I feel free to pick my nose in front of everyone.

We are lucky that Thai people in general are understanding and forgiving, maybe more so than we, the guests. We not only complain about being pointed out daily, "*Farang!*" "*Farang!*" but we women have been especially incensed with Thai women's insistence on calling us fat. Of course we are aware of the stereotype that all Americans are fat and know that statistically Americans have some of the highest percentages of obesity. While a certain percentage of my cohort are a little overweight, every single one of us women, including the fittest of the 20-somethings, have all been called fat. *Uon* is the word in Thai, and of course is another one of those words that stick with us, because we hear it all the time.

It takes some time to understand that calling someone fat doesn't hold the same kind of negative connation in Thailand as it does in the U.S. This is complicated. Thai women don't want to be fat, but it's not rude or necessarily even an insult to call someone fat (to their face!). They are really just calling it like they see it. If I were 20-something, I would surely get a complex. But I'm 30-something, which had given me ample time to come to terms with my body. But considering how small Thai people are in general, of course we all seem fat to them. Furthermore, after the angry, homesick, irritated culture shock phase one experiences in a new country, you come to a phase called "Acceptance," where you learn to, well, accept things about the culture that seemed unacceptable before. You just come to an understanding that it is what it is.

They are getting bigger, however. If I were a betting woman, I'd say it was the milk. Similar to the dairy campaign in the U.S to get people to drink more milk because it's so "healthy," Thais have recently bought into the idea they should drink lots of milk. It's now even provided at school for free. What I see as a result is some young girls who carry extra weight and start to develop at younger and younger ages. Some of the middle school girls have gotten really big, like 5'8" or 5'9", in a country where the average height is closer to 5'.

Of course, like in every country, you see more heavy women as they get older. But rather than feeling fat-shamed, these women seem to own it. A rotund teacher at my school will joke with me later in my service, "*Uon, dta soiay.*" Referring to us both, it means, fat, but beautiful. And while I've been called fat countless times already, I've never been called ugly. That, I believe, would be an insult, and rude, even in Thailand.

At least riding the bicycle everywhere will help take those extra pounds off. Unlike many Europeans, riding a bicycle is not how Thai people choose to get around. For one, it's so freaking hot, one would be crazy to actually partake in an activity that produces even more sweat. Thai people insist on staying clean. Perspiration is avoided. It's also an issue of status in a very class-conscious society. Kids ride bicycles. And stupid foreigners.

The most common mode of transportation for Thai people, even the children, is the motorcycle, or as the Thai people so endearingly call it, the "moto-cy." Often several at a time. None wearing helmets. I can honestly say I don't think I've ever seen a Thai person wear a helmet when riding a motorcycle. One of the craziest sights I'd ever see was a whole family on a motorcycle at the same time, including a few kids and grandma, the littlest perched way up front on the handlebars. Of a motorcycle!!!

Forbidden to drive or even ride on the back of a motor-cycle, even with a helmet, we rely on our trusty bicycles to go everywhere. Therefore, I ended up spending a considerable amount of my Peace Corps service seated on a bicycle. Adventures were bound to ensue.

Every morning, dressed in a skirt, button down shirt and sandals, I ride my bicycle to the school where I am training. The riding path to school is a hazardous obstacle course of mangy dogs, skinny cats, squawking chickens, lizards, and my favorite, all sizes of children. The children run out to the path when they see me and yell, "Hello!" I'm a sweaty mess by the time I arrive at the school. If I venture out later, when I'm freer, in casual clothes, I make sure to return home before the sun starts to set. If not, the bugs have come out so thick they get in your eyes as you're riding.

The days we have to meet in town for whole-group training, I not only have to ride my bicycle in my skirt and sandals, but I have to haul my bicycle down an embankment, lift it onto a "ferry" in order to cross the river, then haul it back up the embankment on the other side. It's hard on my body. I never fail to get scrapes on legs and arms. I usually feel like I've pulled something.

As mentioned before, I'm not a fearful person. No fear of heights whatsoever. I can't wait to jump out of an airplane one day. I give blood regularly, because I am fine with needles. Public speaking? I am one of the few who enjoys it! But like Superman had his kryptonite, I do have one weakness. Snakes terrify me. I will let a spider crawl on me, have been known to rescue spiders and other bugs by lifting them gently in my hand and placing them in a safe spot outdoors. The mere thought of a snake, however, makes me want to ball up in the fetal position in some corner.

The reader surely knows what coming next. I'm living in Thailand. Snakes are a given. But one day as I rode along the raised cement river path with jungle-like greenery on both sides, I witnessed a snake crossing the path. The snake was so big and was moving so slowly that it took me seemingly forever to register what it was. Perhaps it was the just the shock. Either way, I couldn't stop my bike until I was within an inch of it. I was less than a second away from running into it. For there would have been no running over it. It was that big. By the powers of all that is good in the world, as I froze in shock, heart pounding, breathing heavily, that snake just slowly kept going and made its way across the path until it was gone. I was so relieved I wanted to cry. My legs were shaking so bad I couldn't get back on the bicycle seat to ride home. But since there was no corner in which I could roll up in the fetal position, I walked the bike home, keeping my eyes glued on the path ahead of me for as far as I could see.

Almost worse was the time I was riding into town, clipping along at a good pace, when a couple of children ran out to the road to say hello, with their dog following along, barking angrily, surpassing the children. As I looked down I thought, maybe I should lift up my leg, just as the dog proceeded to grab the meat on my left calf between its jaws. It seemed to be happening in slow motion as I thought to myself, "Oh, shit. This feels like skin breaking. This is probably not good." I briefly considered removing my foot from the pedal and kicking the dog in the head, but I was afraid the dog would manage to get a hold of my mostly bare, sandal-wearing foot. So I pedaled faster and the dog let go and I was mad as hell because I always trust the dogs around the village even though I've been told countless times how dangerous Thai dogs can be. I feel betrayed! I'm so disappointed that my trust has been so blatantly taken advantage of. I may never trust a Thai dog again! Unless it's really, really cute.

When I got to town and discovered that yes, indeed, the skin was punctured in about three places, the powers that be at Peace Corps training made me go to the hospital and get yet another freakin' rabies shot. And I have to go back in three days for a follow-up rabies shot. I've already received three rounds of rabies shots. During this time of our training we learn that there are 10 million dogs in Thailand to 70 million people, which brings me to question 1) Who counted all those dogs? 2) Is it possible fewer dogs are found up north where people eat dog? 3) Why haven't these people heard of doggy birth control? We also learned about snakes and are told not to worry too much about snakes, all the while showing us a picture of a guy whose arm is completely void of any skin as a result of a snake bite. I do worry about a snake bite, but not rabies. I'm not foaming at the mouth yet, and I'm sure that dog wasn't rabid. He was just mean.

When I went to the hospital and, speaking Thai, told the nurse that my mother had bitten me, they looked a little shocked. The words for "mother" and "dog" in Thai are very, very, similar. But when they saw how low the teeth marks were on my leg, I think they figured it out. I hope so anyways.

My Thai mother is a very nice person and I'd hate to ruin her reputation like that. I mean, I guess she's been known to talk bad about other people in the neighborhood, but nothing like this.

Bicycle ferry.

Chapter 8

Mark, Moles, and Monkeys

I HAVE BEEN INVITED on an outing with Mark and his host family, who are my next door neighbors in our training village. This is one of the many outings on which I will go that I have no idea where I am going, what I am doing, or how long I will be gone. For someone who has always been a little anal in their need to have plans, this becomes a two-year lesson in ambiguity.

When I first meet Mark's host family, about the youngest, the translator said, "His name means 'Little Penis.'" I kid you not. Put that on my list of things I never thought I'd hear. It also means "inexperienced one." My guess is he's going to go with that. Especially as he gets older.

As usual, Mark and I ride in the back of the truck with three of his host family little brothers. The toddler, "Little Penis," gets to ride in the front with his parents. By this time I've gotten used to riding in the back of the truck with the little brothers and whoever else might be riding along. One night I counted nine of us all crammed under that canopy like sardines, so I'm comfortable with this travel arrangement. In fact, I have discovered that I learn Thai language best from Mark's little brothers while riding in the back of the truck. From them we learn the most impolite expressions, what we would deem "potty talk" in the U.S. For example, the brothers have taught us how to say "fart" in Thai. Unfortunately, the word for fart is almost identical to the word for table. So when our Thai language teacher tries to teach us the word for table, and we keep saying "fart," I fear the poor guy is going to hurt himself for laughing so hard.

I'm more concerned by what the little brothers are learning from us. It's a little unnerving to hear children who speak no other English exclaiming, "Oh my god! Oh my god!" We try to work on some other English phrases for them during the ride today.

When we stop for lunch I'm impressed to see and hear Mark talk about the menu in Thai with his family. Mark's mother is Thai and his grandmother actually lives in Thailand, so he's had some advantage in the language learning. He tells me he's asking them to order his favorite fish dish.

Fish in Thailand is always delicious. Always. But as noted before, the heads are rarely removed, nor are the bones. So one must be careful when delighting in the delectable white flesh. After lunch when we return to the back of the truck, Mark confesses that he's managed to lodge a small, soft fishbone in his throat. If you've had this experience, you know it's not painful, but annoying as hell. The bone doesn't actually puncture the flesh, but sticks to through the top layer of skin. You feel it tickling, or scraping, irritating. Almost like having an itch that you can't scratch, only worse.

I carry tweezers. Always. As a woman of a certain age, I never know when one of those god-awful black hairs is going to sprout from a mole or randomly on my chin. I am compulsive about plucking these hairs, despite the fact that Thai people proudly display their hair-infested moles. Really. It's a thing. I think it's good luck or something. So Thai faces often include a mole sprouting one, two, three or more long black hairs like a garden. The thing is, I can NOT look away when I see one of those things. Like Mike Meyers in Austin Powers, when he first meets the character with the big mole and can't refrain from shouting, "MOLEY MOLEY MOLEY MOLEY MOLEY!" And it's almost impossible to resist the temptation not to whip out my trusty tweezers and relieve the mole of its garden of hairs.

The tweezers prove to be especially handy in the back of the truck as I attempt to perform fishbone-removal surgery on Mark's throat. It takes many, many attempts and what seems like an eternity with Mark's head resting in my lap, the little brothers cheering us on in a mixture of surprise and horror. Considering the taboos around open mouths which should not be exposed to anyone except the dentist, add in that men and women aren't even supposed to touch each other if they're not married. And here I am with my hand in this man's mouth whose head is in my lap. Those poor boys are going to need therapy.

Finally, success! I am able to grasp the elusive bone with the tweezers and free Mark's throat from the irritant.

When we arrive at our destination and we are released from the back of the truck, the little brothers eagerly try to tell the story of the on-the-move "operation." The parents look at us questioningly, but we shrug in ignorance, as if we have no idea what they're talking about. The parents roll their eyes and basically tell the boys they don't know what they're talking about.

It turns out we've been taken to Lop Buri, a town famous for being overrun with monkeys. Literally. Mostly they inhabit the ruins of the 700-year-old palace that is the secondary tourist attraction, after the monkeys. Monkeys are everywhere. They are in the streets. They are in the trees. They are on top of cars, on window ledges, on rooftops, and even on telephone wires. And they are MEAN monkeys! They bite. They even steal. I managed to escape unscathed but somehow, the two-year old little brother got left alone for a second and a monkey attacked him! Luckily, the only harm done was psychological. Especially considering that periodically for the rest of the day his mother would get in his face and pretend to be a monkey to scare him again.

Thanks to a little something on the bottom of another brother's shoe, I've learned how to say monkey poop.

Chapter 9

"Good Morning, Teeeeee-chah"

EVERYTHING I'VE OBSERVED IN THE THAI SCHOOL conveys a highly-disciplined, tightly run ship. These are the most well-mannered, respectful, obedient children I have ever seen. They wait outside the room until given permission to enter. They stay standing at their seats for the morning greeting.

"Good morning, teeeee-chah."

They patiently await instruction to sit down, at which time they respond in unison, "Thank you, teeeeee-chah."

I spend a lot of time with Thai children outside of the classroom and know they are as naughty little hellions outside of class as children anywhere. It doesn't take long to see why they are so well-behaved in class. The teacher gives them a good smack if they aren't.

My first impressions of teachers in Thailand is that they are a professional lot, taking pride in their role as shapers of their country's future. They appear to take their job seriously, work hard, and conscientiously. Sometimes things aren't as they seem.

The longer I'm here, the more I see that being a teacher in Thailand is a pretty cushy gig. You can leave the classroom whenever you want, for as long as you want. You can nap whenever you want. One of the teachers at this particular school shows up drunk every day and no one seems to have a problem with it. I keep trying to imagine what would happen if I showed up in my high school classroom one day, lay back in my chair, put my feet up on my desk, and fell asleep. Better yet, what if I showed up drunk? Of course this was all way before the movie "Bad Teacher."

In Thailand this behavior is possible only because the students are trained to be so responsible. And by trained, I mean spanked, swatted, paddled, or beat into submission. There's a saying in Thailand, "If you love your child, you hit your child." I'll tell you one thing I've learned, abhorrent as it is for any adult to hit a child, let alone for a teacher to do so, it sure makes for an obedient class of kids. Thai teachers have no discipline problems. I worry that I will have discipline problems when I start to teach at my site because I won't be smacking any kids and they will figure that out quickly as kids are wont to do.

As of yet, we are still training for our on-site volunteer service, but are starting to teach more and more in the classroom. I became a high school teacher specifically because I did not want to teach elementary aged students. Therefore I'm surprised to find how much I enjoy doing The Hokey Pokey in a circle of identically dressed Thai children, at first anyway. The students love it so much we do it every day. Another favorite is "Heads, Shoulders, Knees and Toes." The faster we go, the harder they laugh, and the worse their English gets. But we sure have fun!

Alas, my tolerance for The Hokey Pokey is short-lived. I've moved on to "If You're Happy and You Know It." Now that they know the English words for happy, sad and angry, every afternoon when it's time for me to leave, they make mock crying faces, wiping their eyes, and tell me, "I sad! I sad!" Okay, so I'm failing them on the English lesson, but how cute is that!

* * *

Thailand has three seasons. The hot season, the rainy season, and the "cold" season, cold being a blatantly relative term in this case. Our Peace Corps in-country training began in January, which is the middle of the cold season. Coming from wintry, cold northern climes, the "coldness" of January in Thailand feels downright delightful to us. The mornings start off in the very comfortable 60s. The afternoon highs of mid-80s feel a bit too hot to us.

As January turns to February and we get closer to March, we are entering the hot season, with April being the hottest. No quotation marks required for the "hot". Now it's officially hot. I mean, really, really hot, like over 100 degrees every day hot. It's ridiculously uncomfortable.

The average Thai house isn't air-conditioned. Thai people complain about the hot weather just as much as we Americans. However, they have tried and true methods to deal with the heat. Number one, the splash bath. I wonder if Thai people really value cleanliness, or if they bathe so much because it feels so good to cool off with a good old-fashioned Thai splash bath. When you've been riding your bicycle in the heat of the day and you are panting, hot and sweaty, and you come home, the first thing you do is go straight into the bathroom and douse yourself with bucket after bucket of the delectably cool water. Ahhhh. With each new bucket filled and poured over your head, your temperature comes down, refreshed. Nothing beats the feeling of the heat releasing from your body. It's heaven.

Another tried and true way to keep cool, which is now my new best friend, is powder. As in talc. Of course this was years before we learned the associations between talcum powder and cancer, so at the time, powder was king. I have learned from Thai people to use powder liberally. After every bath-by-bucket I smooth it all over my body, especially under my arms and boobs. I even smooth some on my cheeks, which seemed weird at first, but hey, everyone else is doing it. When in Rome, and all that.

Schools aren't air-conditioned, except for the principal's office. (How well would THAT go over in the U.S.?) To keep them cool, the little ones get powdered up each afternoon. After lunch they all stand in line and one-by-one the teacher rubs talc on each face. Then they run off to play. With those white powdered faces they look startlingly like little ghosts running around. See? Ghosts everywhere in Thailand.

Powder helps with the heat, as do the splash baths, but knowing I will have to ride my bicycle everywhere when I get to my site, often in the heat of the day, in a skirt and button down shirt no less, I come up with a plan to stay cool. A plan better than powder.

Supposedly, volunteers have a say in where they will be placed for their volunteer service. I will request a work site up north where it's mountainous and milder and pretend it's a former Soviet country. Maybe I can find a fur-lined coat. Doubtful, but maybe.

Chapter 10

New Site, New Sight

I THINK MOST OF US have this image of Peace Corps volunteers living in thatched-roof huts with dirt floors, no indoor plumbing or electricity, having to walk to the local well for water, using an outhouse. That's the image I had anyways. However, before I came to Thailand, I read somewhere that there was a good chance the home I'd get at my work site would have electricity and running water. What a relief!

The truth is, Thailand has somewhat of a reputation within the international Peace Corps community. Unlike many of the Third World nations in which volunteers serve, in places like Africa, or South America, where living conditions are truly rustic, Thailand is considered a rare Peace Corps placement of luxury. There's even a name for it: Posh Corps.

I almost wonder if, as part of the Peace Corps screening process, they determine who the biggest weenies are, the ones who wouldn't be able to handle a "real" Peace Corps experience, and send them to Thailand.

As we eagerly await our site placement assignments the discussion among the volunteers sounds like this:

"I could definitely live without a water heater, but not without screens on my windows."

"I won't take a house that doesn't have air-conditioning AND a water heater."

"I'm okay without air-conditioning, but I'm definitely having laundry service."

"I might get a TV and VCR." That would have to be with

one's own savings of course, because our living stipend only allows for a certain amount of luxuries.

Mind you, discussion of a Western-style toilet didn't even occur because not having one is just a given.

In all fairness, several volunteers do hope for and seek out the most challenging living conditions. They are what I call "Hard Core Peace Corps." I am not one of them.

Then at last! We finally receive our site placements! I learn where I will live and work for the next two years of my Peace Corps service in Thailand! Was it up north where it's beautiful mountainous and cool? This is what I requested and several volunteers will be placed there. Was it down south at one of the beach sites? That would be nice too and several volunteers get to look forward to that! It could be one of those places!

Spoiler alert. It wasn't. I will be living in the northeast, where it's hot, where there are no mountains, where there are no beaches, not even much green. I'm sure it will have its own charms.

I take a deep breath and remind myself, despite the moniker Posh Corps, this is actually the Peace Corps, the toughest job I'll ever love. (I don't think the creative mind behind that slogan was a parent). I remind myself this is supposed to be hard and remember that idealism of embracing the hardship. I can do this! It's going to be amazing, no matter what my site is.

Secretly, I'm a little heart broken.

The good news is that I passed my oral language examination. At least I thought it was good news. I studied my ass off AND fed the monks for good merit, only to learn that the 11 people who didn't pass get extra help. Dammit! I would have loved the opportunity for extra help. Why-oh-why did I study so hard? Curse me and my need to always succeed academically. Had I known the consequence for failing was extra help I could have played dumb. Then again, if I passed with my very limited language ability, how bad do you have to speak Thai to fail?

In one of the "Meet the Parents" movies, Owen Wilson has a line to Ben Stiller, "Todd talk Thai. Todd talk Thai real good." It's hilarious. And since one of the volunteers' names is Todd, and since he happens to be at the top of the class for Thai language, well, you can imagine. We've gotten a lot of mileage with that movie reference. We've also created another phrase, to describe some of the rest of us. "No talk Thai. No talk Thai at all."

You know that joke Americans have about Asians pronouncing "fried rice" as "flied lice"? Well now the jokes on us. Dog comes out as mom. Table comes out as fart. I heard one volunteer was trying to teach students about snow, and it came out sounding like "dog's vagina." I can only imagine the trouble in which I might find myself. God I hope my Thai counterparts at my work site speak English!

Before we finish training and move to our official site, we'll make an introductory visit to said site. We'll meet our co-teachers and other Thai partners, look for possible houses, learn our way around the village or, in my case, a town called Non Sung. We'll get introduced to the people of the town and become acquainted with what will be our homes for the next two years.

I'm told the charms of northeast Thailand, where I will live, are its culture, people, and hospitality. To me, that sounds a little too much like when someone wants to set you up with a guy, and you ask what he looks like, and he's described as having "a great personality." One can assume the guy isn't considered very physically attractive. I'd probably fall for the better looking, sexy, but much shallower best friend. So, ashamed as I am to acknowledge it, what excites me the most about my new site is its proximity to Bangkok, about three hours or so by bus. Not to mention, my small town of Non Sung is only about 20 minutes away from the large city of Korat where supposedly one can find amenities appealing to a Westerner, i.e. pizza, cheese, lettuce salad, and other luxuries. Score!

So far my experience with Thai people is that unless they work for Peace Corps, their English is about where my Thai is, limited to none. Therefore, with the glass-half-empty attitude I'm prone to, I am not hopeful that my Thai counterparts in Non Sung and I will be able to communicate at all. I do, however, trust that eventually my Thai skills will allow me to communicate as much as needed. Spoiler alert. They don't.

Traveling to my site on my own, despite the training, was humbling to say the least. The ticket people don't understand what I say. I don't understand what they say to me. You just have to swallow your pride and suck it up, and ask yourself, "What's the worst thing that can happen?" Well, I could get lost. (I didn't, but one volunteer did. He ended up in a completely different town in the completely opposite direction. I refrained from making any jokes about men and refusing to ask for directions.)

I managed to make it to the bus station in Korat, where, waiting for my Thai counterparts and wondering how's this gonna go down, I have an "aha" moment. It dawns on me, I'm not nearly as nervous as I was that day just three weeks ago when I met my host family. Could this be a sign of growth? Have I become more resilient? Or have I simply just had enough experience to know what the worst things that can happen are, and thus I am prepared. I know that if you can't communicate, you can smile and nod awkwardly for however long needed. You can point. You can also pull out your handy-dandy English-Thai dictionary. I take a deep breath and smile to myself because I know I can do this.

Still, imagine my shock and relief when I'm greeted at the bus station by a stylish, Thai woman in a short skirt and high heels who says to me plain as day in English, "Are you Amy?

Welcome. I'm so glad you're here!" If you're wondering how she knew it was me, you're forgetting this part of Thailand is home to very few Westerners, or as my friend Mark and I refer to them affectionately, "Whiteys." The few farangs, or whiteys who do live in this province, are retired men, often former military, who have found much younger Thai wives. Furthermore, in case it wasn't made clear in my earlier description, this is not exactly a tourist destination. Therefore, I am the one and only white person in the bus station making it quite clear who to approach.

She grabs me by the arm, and walks me to the principal and director who are so pleased and impressed that I know how to say hello and that I *wai* (bow with hands folded in greeting), that I feel almost accomplished. It's encouraging that they have such low expectations.

The cute, high-heeled woman is Somjai, my co-teacher, the woman with whom I've been partnered by Peace Corps to help improve education in Thailand. Clearly, she is fluent in English. I can hardly contain my joy. After my disappointment with this site placement and everyone assuring me that something will make up for it, I realize something. Even if I were in the most beautiful, exotic location with a cool, comfortable climate as I'd hoped, I would probably still suffer from a mental breakdown and have to come home early for therapy if I were working with only non-English speaking people for two years. Terrible, but true. Thus I feel most fortunate and am glad I fed the monks and made other offerings to the Buddha.

My feelings of good fortune only multiply. Not only does Somjai speak fluent English, but inexplicably I feel completely comfortable and at ease with her. She seems almost familiar to me. Like a long lost friend.

The first thing Somjai asks is my age. As rude as that seems from my own culture, I know that it's crucial information to know when interacting with others in Thailand. The whole society is based on a hierarchy, called the "*pi* (pronounced 'pee') *nong*" system. One uses the "*pi*" or "*nong*" prefix when addressing each other. Especially the "*pi*", as it signifies the older of the two people. When used with one's nickname, as all Thai people have, it is a sign of endearment. While age holds great honor, almost a religious reverence, age is not the only factor in the hierarchy. Status in education, salary, or job title are considered as well. Status also dictates other social behavior, such as who has to pay when you go out to eat. (Thais find "going Dutch" utterly incomprehensible. The higher-up always, always pays for everyone.)

Therefore, it's not impolite to ask someone how old they are, how much money they make, and my personal favorite, asked by my host father, "How many acres do you own?" These questions help them put you in your correct social category according to their hierarchy.

These very direct questions, along with "Why aren't you married?" and statements such as "you're fat" imply a direct society. This implication is incorrect, causing great confusion for the foreigner. In fact, despite these exceptions to the rule, Thais prefer an indirect communication style for which we volunteers are trained. For example, if you try a food that you find utterly disgusting, instead of saying you don't like it, you should say, "it's a little delicious." It gets the point across while saving face. Instead of saying "no" to an invitation, one should always provide some excuse, usually not true, again in order to save face for the other person. More often, one should actually just accept, for the sake of *grang jai*. Literally translated as "generous heart," it's the concept of doing what you don't want to because it's the nice thing to do. It's one I'll struggle with, and often fail at, for the next two years.

I learn that Somjai, despite her sexy legs and youthful appearance, is about 10 years older than me, with a daughter in college. I will forever envy Thai women's ability to age so well. She is my "*pi*." Her nickname, by which almost all Thais go in their close circle, is Noi, which means "little". Therefore, I should address her as Pi Noi. I will also come to learn that this woman is actually very direct even compared to American standards. She's an exception to the rule and somewhat of an aberration in Thailand. This bodes well for me. For the most part.

When the director takes us all out to dinner, I find him quite a jovial and enjoyable character despite his limited English. To improve his English, he intends to speak only English to me, while I'm instructed to speak only Thai to him. About me he says, "*Mai chai farang, kon Thai.*" It means he doesn't view me as a foreigner, but as a Thai person. I take it as a great welcome, for although farang isn't necessarily an insult, it definitely connotes "outsider."

Since one of northeast Thailand's charms is its unique cuisine with its Lao influence, I'm treated to several of the local specialties. No need for the "It's a little delicious" here. One question foreigners are automatically always asked by Thais is "Can you eat hot (spicy) food?" The perception is that we can't. I assure them I love spicy food and impress them again with my ability to eat and enjoy it. I will spend the next two years impressing every Thai with whom I eat with my ability to not only eat spicy food, but to outspice most of them.

Somjai says that when I live here we won't eat dinner at all. Instead, we will go to aerobics class together every night, because "we want a slender volunteer." Agh, again with the fat comments! Oh well. It is what it is. Or, as they say in Thailand, "*Mai pen rai.*" Never mind. Let it go. It is what it is.

As a special treat, she takes me for a mani/pedi at the local beauty shop where I also had my hair shampooed and blow dried, all for a whopping 70 baht, which is less than

$2.00 American. Unbelievable. While I was having my toe-nails painted, a man with an elephant came to the door of the shop. He wanted 10 baht for me to feed the elephant. Foreigners are usually a sure bet on this. And since the elephant was small and looked so sad I wanted to pay to feed her. But I was in the middle of my pedicure. Next time I vow to feed the elephant.

My first morning, after spending the night at the principal's house, I'm taken to the sports yard of the school where I'm introduced. To the whole school. About 200 students and all the teachers. One can imagine this sort of introduction, right? What questions might I expect to be asked? "Where are you from?" "What do you think of Thailand?" "Do you like Thai food?" or maybe just "Tell us something about yourself."

No. Instead they ask me, in front of 200-some students, "Do you have a boyfriend?" and hand me the microphone. Awkward pause…. "No." Hands covering mouths as students giggle, whisper to each other, pointing at me conspiratorially.

Still, boyfriend or no, I am an instant celebrity at the school. Literally. Turns out a farang in this town is a really big deal. I end up giving over 100 autographs to students from grades K-9. A couple of older girls approached me and spoke in their practiced English, "Teacher is beautiful" and "You are pretty very much." This almost makes up for all the fat comments. I realize with some guilt and sadness that my attractiveness to them is basically about my white skin. In this brown skinned country, white skin is revered. All stores carry skin lightening products which are advertised unabashedly on TV. The principal of my school even told me how sad her daughter is to have dark skin, how sad her father is because she inherited it from him. I'm white, therefore I'm beautiful. I find this focus on white skin and this distorted idea of beauty a travesty and will struggle with this cultural reality for the next two years.

For the time I ignore my guilt, as all this positive attention is a boost to my ego and confidence and taps into my "star" quality. I've always considered myself humble and self-deprecating, but make no mistake, this goes straight to my head. Who knew I would enjoy fame and stardom? Who knew I was so vain? For when it comes time to be introduced to the village people, and I mean literally, the whole village comes out to this event, I am displayed on a huge stage, and, believe it or not, asked to sing a song. While I feign modesty, my ego and vanity are quite pleased.

I can carry a tune, barely, but do not have what's considered a "good" voice. By this time I have heard enough Thai singing and witnessed enough karaoke to I know that having a good voice doesn't matter one lick. What's important is the star quality. That, dear reader, I have.

As a child I loved nothing more to perform pantomimes to pop music, my best being "American Pie" by Don McClean. I forced my whole family (I have five older sisters and one older brother) to come downstairs and sit as my audience as I put the needle on the 45 record and acted out how "February made me shiver, with every paper I delivered." I was a middle school cheerleader where I choreographed half-time shows for my very, very small, but very big on basketball school. I loved the spotlight. In high school I had a very, very small role in my church's performance of the musical "Bye Bye Birdie." Finally, and by a fluke, because the drama teacher position was paired with the English teaching position for which I was hired, I became, by default, a drama teacher, where I took on adult roles on the stage with my students. Star quality, I tell you!

Never mind all the preconceived notions of the hardships of the Peace Corps volunteer. You know those images of dirty, sweaty young people digging wells, planting trees, building schools. No. I am on a stage wearing a dress and lipstick in front of hundreds of "fans." It's almost surreal, like being on Fantasy Island, where you get to live out some secret dream, only I never knew being a star was a dream of mine. Of course this was before "American Idol," but in retrospect, this is the perfect title. I bow when they applaud at the end. They love me! They really, really love me!

The reader might be wondering, what song, pray tell, did I sing? Well, all those karaoke experiences taught me there are certain "old school" American songs that are very popular in Thailand. One such song, happens to be an old family favorite of mine. When I was a child of six or seven, my guitar playing sisters and I sang it over, and over, and over. I'm referring to the John Denver classic, "Take me Home, Country Roads." This is the song I chose, since I know every word by heart (I'm not provided a screen with lyrics on my stage).

I get so caught up in my stardom, I don't even notice how the lyrics of this song are all wrong for someone who has just been welcomed into a new country. Much later, after many

On stage.

such performances of this song on a stage at similar events in my town, I do realize this is not the message I want to send and I'll change my song to The Carpenters' "Sing a Song," another Thai favorite. By then, they've grown to love my John Denver rendition so much that they are disappointed when I change it. Later still it dawns on me that very few of those people had a clue what the words in "Take Me Home Country Roads" meant anyway.

* * *

Before I leave, Somjai and I have a discussion about Buddhism, karma and reincarnation. Somjai tells me we have shared a past life together. I guess this sense of meeting a long lost friend was mutual.

Chapter 11

The End of the Beginning

Letter to my sister Shannon:

Dear Shannon, I feel like it's been a while since I've heard anything from you and I hope no news is good news. Maybe "Survivor Amazon" has just gotten too disappointing to you to share about. But at least there's still Jeff Probst. Now that's a man I miss! Actually, I miss a lot. I miss you, mom and dad, tacos, anything familiar and comfortable. Sometimes I want to come home. But I know the feeling comes and goes. Don't tell mom and dad, but the front page of the newspaper here says that if the U.S. goes to war with Iraq, Southeast Asia (Thailand) will be the first place terrorists strike out against Americans. We've been given a detailed account of the emergency plan. Don't worry. I don't. Once we get to site we will be very safe because each of us will be the only American for miles. But I do worry about you and your MS. I worry about mom. You know her memory seemed very, very bad on that last trip we took. Please keep in touch! Those care packages you mentioned before? I haven't received any of them yet. So looking forward to getting them! Miss you! Give my love to everyone! Love, Amy

AFTER A MONTH OF TRAINING LIMBO, having no idea where I would live the next two years of my life…now I know. Being able to visualize the place, the people I'll work with every day, a new kind of excitement for the adventures to come sets in. Then reality hits hard. The Peace Corps umbilical cord is being severed awfully abruptly. Or for a more aesthetic metaphor, the mother bird Peace Corps is kicking the baby birds right out of the nest. Only three more weeks of training.

While much of this training and orientation experience has been difficult, for the most part, Peace Corps staff and our host families have taken care of us. My guess is we have no idea about how difficult or challenging this experience can be until we get to our site and have to fend for ourselves. Our host mother won't be there to prepare all of our meals. No aunties to make sure we hang our laundry correctly. We won't have our bilingual language teachers with us at school every day to help translate. Scariest for me, we won't have each other, the other Peace Corps volunteers, with whom to vent, drink, joke, reminisce, or just speak English. For we haven't yet had a true immersion experience. We've had "Little America" in our village.

With just these few weeks left here, I pause to reflect. I have many regrets. Even though it was arguably necessary for my survival, I regret spending so much time alone in my room instead of practicing Thai language with my host family. I spent too much time whining about my uncomfortable bed, complaining about the heat, judging moles and nose picking, bitching about noisy roosters. I spent too little time savoring the magic and the amazing wonders of the experience. I vow to savor these last days in my sleepy village, where my bike path along the river abounds with a feast for the senses, sounds, scents, and lush jungle green of the huge palm leaves of banana trees. The setting sun itself turns brilliant pink into red.

I've learned how deep of a bond one can make with no language whatsoever. I can count on two hands how many different words I used with auntie #2. Yet I grew to love her.

My host mother too. So much shared with a smile, a gesture. Words may not even be the best form of communication. I've learned there's a certain freedom without the ability to use language. You never worry about saying the wrong thing. I can understand how farang men can be in relationships with Thai women when they don't speak the same language. But maybe that's just me, an introvert who often prefers to say nothing, who has always been overly self-conscious and prone to social anxiety. That is, except when I'm on a stage.

* * *

Before we leave for site, all of the volunteers buy cell phones. While I had only recently acquired one back in the U.S., in the year 2003 they are prolific in Thailand, used by almost everyone. They are inexpensive and, instead of a Verizon, or AT&T "plan" with a contract and monthly charge, everyone buys pay-as-you go cards that you can purchase in every 7-11 or other convenience store in Thailand.

The term "minutes" becomes ubiquitous in our conversations. We buy minutes. We run out of minutes. We only have x amount of minutes left. Like so much of my experience in Thailand thus far, this doesn't fit my image of a Peace Corps volunteer. I imagined I'd be riding my bike to the town's one and only pay phone to make my one budgeted phone call for the week. Instead, almost every day I ride my bike to one of the town's many internet shops where I send and receive emails, charged about 50 cents by the hour. This is before Facebook and if the internet is used for news or research, I'm not yet versed in this practice. I find email connection a complete and utter luxury. Along with my new cell phone. It's comforting to know that once we live in our work sites we'll have this connection to the other volunteers and even home in the U.S., for a price. Years later when Facebook, Youtube,

Line, Whatsapp, Skype, and other forms of social media are globally pervasive, I'll wonder how that impacts the life of a Peace Corps volunteer.

From the young members of my cohort I learn about a new way to communicate using the phone called "texting." It's cheaper to text than to actually call. The young people in my cohort are all familiar with this new technology and promise to teach me how to do it.

That night I receive my first ever text message. It says, "Good night Amy." I smile. I'm going to like texting.

Chapter 12

There's Thailand. Then there's Bangkok.

STATISTICALLY, 10% OF ALL PEACE CORPS VOLUNTEERS will not even make it through training. Statistics shamistics! With just a few days left of training, we are all still here! (Knock on wood. And I've been crossing my fingers as well as making merit with monks and praying to Buddha.) My eye is on the end date, our Swearing-In ceremony, which is to take place in…Bangkok.

Bangkok! We have heard so much about that city. It's understood by everyone living in Thailand and visitors alike. It's as if there are two different entities; there's Thailand, and then there's Bangkok. Unlike our training villages and the sites where we'll complete our service, Bangkok is a First World, multi-cultural city with all the modern amenities we've gone without for these two months. Hot water. Air-conditioning. English channels on the TV. Cheeseburgers and fries! The first place I'm going to go when I get to Bangkok is McDonald's. A woman has needs. Don't judge me.

My last nights at my training site are booked solid with party after party after party. We attend another monk-becoming. This one is a crazy-big party, with over 500 guests. I now understand that these monk-becomings are a really big deal to the family because of the honor and respect bestowed on monks in Thai society. Monks are prestigious, second only to the king in the hierarchy. A monk-becoming is not a life-long commitment, but a three-month commitment young men make to bring honor to their family as much as anything. Despite the religious cause for this celebration, everyone gets drunk, except the poor young monk who, instead, has to go around to every one of the 50 tables and get his picture taken.

I'm embarrassed to admit this, but I found myself inexplicably attracted to the monk, his sculpted features, strong, high cheekbones, shaved eyebrows, skin the color of a café latte. Surely romantic attraction to a monk is wrong! Sacrilegious. Still, I find myself wanting to rub oil on his tawny bald head, like in the Seinfeld episode where George gets intimate with the Jamaican housekeeper who loves to rub oil on his bald head. This is only one of the many of my Peace Corps experiences that recall a Seinfeld episode.

Our final pep talk in training includes a reality check about how we'll have the freedom to choose how to spend our time. We'll be tempted to stay in our room alone with books (in English) and CDs. But we have to buck up and remember why we're here. The second goal of Peace Corps is to foster friendship. Therefore we must immerse ourselves in our communities and spend time IRBing (Intentional Relationship Building). It's also the only way we'll determine our secondary project, one chosen by us based on the needs of our communities, one that's sustainable. Peace Corps training is nothing if not clear on the importance of IRBing and sustainability.

I make a silent vow to try my best, secretly a little unsure of what my "best" will allow me to do.

*   *   *

Arriving at our hotel in Bangkok where the Swearing-In ceremony will occur, we're like kids arriving at Disneyland. I know I said the first thing I was going to do was go to McDonalds, but the first thing I do is take a hot bath, my first in two months. A complete and utter luxury. If I take nothing else from this experience it will be to never ever take modern comforts for granted. Is that why people go camping?

Our hotel rooms have these huge drawers in which we can't help but be tempted to tuck away our Thai language teachers to sleep in, like in the Seinfeld episode when Kramer makes money by renting out drawers for the Japanese visitors to New York City. We wouldn't take money from our Thai trainers. We don't even need them here because everyone seems to speak English. We just want them close by because we love them so much.

While in Bangkok, I take in not one, not two, but three English language movies at the modern, air-conditioned, pop-corn providing theater. If not for the Thai subtitles at the bottom of the screen, I would forget I'm in Thailand. Oh, and that at the beginning of every movie, the Thai national anthem is played and everyone stands to watch the video of the king[3]. While democracy is alive and well in Thailand in many ways, make no mistake, it's a democratic monarchy. The love, respect and honor for their king is palpable and indisputable. There's no question we will stand. We're pretty sure there'd be trouble if we didn't.

* * *

The Swearing In ceremony is quite formal and somber. The U.S. Ambassador to Thailand tells us to raise our right hand and repeat after him. I've pledged to uphold the Constitution of the United States. Wait, do I even know what's IN the Constitution of the United States? Never mind. This will be

---

3 When King Bhumibol Adulyadej died in 2016, he had reigned for 70 years and therefore was the monarch during every PCV's time in Thailand. He'd done much good for his people. Thais mourned his passing with great sadness.

the first of many formalities I'll go along with as a volunteer in which I have no idea what's going on.

That evening, it's time to celebrate. We made it! Each and every one of us. No longer trainees, we are officially Peace Corps Volunteers a.k.a. PCVs. We desperately need to let off steam, and where better to do that than in the city of Bangkok!

We're joined by members of the PC group who arrived the year before us, as well as some who arrived over two years ago, but chose to extend their service. They take us to Kao San Road.

Kao San Road is a backpacker's paradise. I've never seen anything like it. On this half-mile stretch the street is packed with young (mostly) foreigners, Europeans traveling during their gap year, Australians enjoying the proximity and affordable travel, volunteers letting off steam.

Walking this strip along with this hodgepodge of travelers wearing sweaty t-shirts, hippie skirts made in India, Teva sandals or Birkenstocks, and of course, backpacks, we hear a mix of languages and accents. Here we finally understand why Thais have a stereotype that Westerners are dirty. During training, we defensively explained to our Thai trainers that showering once a day doesn't make us unclean. We don't shower multiple times a day because in our temperate climate, we don't sweat as much. (I don't dare admit that in the winter I don't even shower every day). But seeing (and smelling) the backpackers, we finally get the stereotype and don't take it so personally.

What brings this rag tag set of travelers to Kao San Road? Cheap lodging, backpacker supplies and souvenirs, bars and clubs. Every kind of ethnic food you'd want. The Indian restaurant will become my favorite, seconded by the Israeli. Vendors with stalls hocking bootlegged DVDs and CDs. Knock off bags, sunglasses and clothing. Street vendors serving up all the best Thai food you could want, including a delicous phad thai for less than 50 cents a plate. Icy, refreshing fruit ice concoctions for 10 cents a bag. Yes, a bag. Trust me, the drink served in a plastic bag is brilliantly practical.

Eventually we all end up at a dance club. I had assumed my clubbing days were over. I'm surprised to find that the music and dancing is not so different from 15 years ago, or even 30 years ago, as we groove to a techno version of Donna Summer's "I Feel Love." I let the primitive beat take over my body and release the tensions of the past two months forgetting momentarily that I'm in Thailand, that I'm a Peace Corps volunteer. I'm just another body in a dance club. We're connecting at a primal level, in solidarity, celebrating our accomplishment. I don't even care that I'm the oldest one.

At times I've envied the younger volunteers, jealous of their youth, their self-confidence, their idealism. Other times they reminded me too much of the high school students from whom I fled when I quit teaching to join the Peace Corps. Now I'm filled with respect for each of them. Through the challenges this far, I've learned the stuff they are made of, as I learned my own fortitude. They will represent the U.S. honorably and accomplish much for the people of Thailand.

Although the "older" PCVs are not with us in the dance club, I also pause to reflect on my respect and admiration for the retired volunteers, the couples and singles in their 60s. They serve as an inspiration, proving it's never too late.

The next morning's departures to our sites was bittersweet. Scary. Exciting. Desperately sad. We're going to miss the friends in training to whom we've grown so close over these past two months. Of course we'll see each other again, but when and how often, those are still unknowns. So many unknowns.

* * *

Dear Friends, While in Bangkok for our Swearing-In ceremony, we were gathered together for the somber announcement that President George W. Bush has made the unilateral decision to declare war on Iraq. We were informed about emergency evacuation plans, should the need arise, and assured that our safety was Peace Corps' primary concern.....To those of you who are upset with the president's actions, I want to offer some small consolation. While our government wages war, there are factions all over the world waging peace. We are called Peace Corps volunteers. Our job is to promote peace and foster friendship with other nations. I assure you, as a result of this news, we are more determined than ever to succeed on our mission of peace.

—Mass email to friends and family

Part Two

April 2003 to March 2005

Chapter 13

Home Sweet (Sour, Spicy, Salty) Home

My first night at my site, I'm housed in temporary teacher housing, on the same street as the school, where several of the teachers live. This is a single-roomed, rustic, shack with only a bed and night table for furnishings. I'm glad I don't arrive until bedtime. For the first time since living in Thailand I sleep with a mosquito net. The mosquito net renders my world surreal. More than surreal, it's like a veil to another portal, and this was way, way before "Stranger Things". Surely ghosts reside beyond this veil.

In the middle of the night I wake from yet another dream about aliens, this time behind a veil. Too frightened to go back to sleep, and needing to pee, I venture out of my cocoon. I don't want to leave my bed, but I can't hold it any longer.

I make my way to my "bathroom" which is a dark, dank cement stall with a faucet and bucket and hole in the ground and cobwebs in the ceiling corners. I squat down and start to pee, then, startled, I almost fall over. Dear god and lord have mercy! In the corner, little eyes staring at me. It's a huge bullfrog who has made himself at home on the wet floor in my dark bathroom. He's not a snake, thank god, but he is creepy. I desperately want him out of there, but I'm actually too afraid of him to do that. I won't even attempt to shoo him out. Even though I know this frog is in no way a threat to me, and he has a quite benign look on his face, he freaks me the hell out. Go figure. Add frogs to my list of things

I'm afraid of. Every time I use the toilet he watches me pee, looking a little annoyed that I've encroached on his space. Pervert.

My bathroom.

In the morning, as I prepare to leave for the day, I'm visited by the curious and novelty seeking. Countless children stand outside my window with big smiles, just to say hello and see what the farang is up to. It seems a lot to ask to have to be smiling and friendly to a flock of strangers first thing in the morning, before I've had my coffee, but this is the Peace

Corps. I mount my trusty bicycle and make my way to the market. Despite the sleep deprivation I feel elation to be on my own for the first time in my new town.

Walking through the early morning market, I am the lone white-skinned, blued-eyed, auburn-haired human in a sea of brown-skinned, brown-eyed, black-haired humans. With huge grins on their beautiful faces they call out to me "Aim-EEEE!" I'm reminded why Thailand is known as the "The Land of Smiles." I overhear and understand even with my limited Thai "Amy comes alone." They're as surprised as I'm proud. I smile and say hello to everyone whose eyes I meet as I make my way to the same coffee vendor Somjai took me to when I first visited. I take comfort in any small familiarity. The vendor is happy for my business and asks if I'll have the same as last time. Strong coffee with condensed milk. No sugar. She remembered!

Some people approach me and attempt conversation in Thai. While I have mastered a few basics of the language, or "survival Thai," I still don't understand 99%, which is frustrating and exhausting. Because they heard me introduce myself in Thai on stage, where I recited the memorized "My name is Amy. I am a Peace Corps volunteer. I am from the U.S. I will live here for two years," they think I can speak Thai. They look disappointed when I don't understand them. I'm disappointed in myself, too.

In fact, my plan is to study some Thai while I drink my coffee. Alas, the market is far too stimulating, a virtual feast for the senses and I'm too entranced with the visual stimulation. I marvel at the rainbow colors of the market; reds and purples and every shade of green of the fruits and vegetables. I see shining, shimmering, silver brown fish and eels, sparkling in the sun, some still swimming in bright colored plastic pools of water. Less appealing, but nonetheless visually striking I see maggots, ant larvae, barbequed whole rats skewered on a stick and chicken blood. None of these bother me except the plastic vats of live frogs, thanks to my little (big) roommate and bathroom friend. And yes, everything I've described is for consumption.

Market.

Ironically, for lunch that day and for the first of many times, I'm offered frog as part of the meal. As per my rule of trying everything I'm offered, I do partake in the frog dish. It's not terrible, in fact it tastes like chicken, but I can't get past the image of my bathroom friend. Not to mention the crunch of the bones. Forgetting the "little delicious" etiquette, I tell them we don't eat frog in the US. Although I do end up acquiring a taste for many things, some things you just never get used to. Frog for lunch is one.

After my second cup of coffee, I have one mission, and that is to buy toilet paper. While Thai custom is to use the hand/splash method only, and no Thai bathroom will provide toilet paper, I've learned that it is actually not a problem for the plumbing to put toilet paper down the hole in the ground squat toilet. Hallelujah. I will never leave home without it.

Unfortunately, "What do you want to buy?" sounds a lot like "What is your name?" They ask the former, I answer the latter. We share a good laugh and after proper introductions, because my name is not "toilet paper," they tell me they can arrange to have Bangkok's English language newspaper available at this shop every day. Oh my god, how cool is that! The daily newspaper will give me my English fix and keep me up on current events. I also note that these are clever business women. If I have to come to this shop every day to pick up my newspaper, chances are, that's where I'll do my shopping.

Chapter 14

For the Love of Lizards

Since I did not find a house when I first visited my site, this is a priority on my list of things to do. Somjai is tasked with making this happen. Since Peace Corps has put so much pressure on our Thai counterparts to keep us safe, in conjunction with the Thai compulsion to take care of their guests, Somjai takes this to heart with an almost paranoid zeal. She wants me close. Very close. Too close.

Thai society is very communal. They are a social people who, as a rule, don't like to be alone. Privacy holds no value. I'm not even sure if the concept of privacy can be understood. Since most of the teachers live on the same street as the school, or within walking distance, Somjai is adamant that's the best place for me to live as well.

While Somjai wants me close to keep me safe, I want to keep my sanity. I know exactly what will happen if I take the house across the street from my school. I will have children at my door at all times. I will be THE neighborhood hangout. And I will go crazy. I won't do any good in this community if I go nuts and have to return home early. It happens. We've heard stories. For me it's like the requirement on an airplane to put your own oxygen mask on first. As much as I'd like to fulfill the ideal of that PCV who immerses herself totally in her community with round-the-clock IRBing, I have come to terms with my desperate need for privacy with strong doses of solitude. Despite the fact that living on school grounds would be the best thing for my cultural experience, I adamantly refuse.

The next house she shows me is a little farther away and would be perfect for the "Hard Core Peace Corps." It's like a tree house. Up high on wooden stilts, it has walls and a roof, and nothing else. The little old hunched over woman showing it so desperately wants to rent it that I almost consider. Almost. I'm relieved to know there are some rustic options available for the Hard Core so they don't have to endure too much comfort.

As for me, we'll keep looking. Also on our to-do list today is the hospital. Somjai has been tasked with taking me to the town's hospital and introducing me. Really? I try to imagine having a guest in my town and taking them to the hospital to be introduced. While this seems weird to me, later I will be very, very grateful for this introduction.

Walking into this open aired hospital is like walking straight into the 1950s. The nurses wear old style white nurse uniforms, skirts with white nylon stockings, and their hair tied back under those crisply folded little white hats. We have a picture of my oldest sister wearing that little hat when she graduated from nursing school in 1968! They are only missing the capes.

The man in charge appears to be one Dr. Sombat. Dr. Sombat speaks English almost fluently. Soft-spoken, kind, and ever so polite, Dr. Sombat prefaces every question to me with "Excuse me…". When he learns I'm still looking for a house he has great news. His housekeeper owns a house that they'd like to rent. It's a couple of miles outside of town in a village, or what I'd call a suburb. And it's fully furnished, at least by Thai standards. It's cement with screened windows and shiny, cool, white tile covering the floor. The couch and chairs are the standard hardwood, with no cushions, no upholstery. The bed has a real mattress. It has everything except the kitchen sink! Literally. The kitchen has no sink. However, the bathroom does have a sink with running water. I imagine the Seinfeld episode where Kramer is washing salad in the shower. If I live in this house, I'll be washing all their vegetables in the shower. The bathroom does also have a shower head on the wall, in addition to the prerequisite huge vat of water. No water heater, but hot water is not a priority for me in this tropical climate and I actually love, love, love a cool splash bath in lieu of a hot shower. Technically the toilet is a squat toilet, but this porcelain pedestal is actually raised a good foot off the floor. With my short legs I would have no problem sitting on the raised foot grooves pretending it's a sit toilet. Toilet seats are overrated anyway. And bathroom+bonus! This bathroom includes one of those spray hoses attached to the wall, both hygienic AND refreshing!

This house is perfect to me. But not to Somjai. She insists it's too far from the school, too far from her. She attempts to guilt me about how I am her responsibility and that she promised Peace Corps she'd keep me safe. She thinks the 10-minute bike ride is too much. She begs me, please, please don't take this house.

In the first of what will be many battles of the will between Somjai and me, I win. I assure her the bike ride is great for me as it will make me more slender. I remind her that I've been on my own in the U.S. for many years and managed to survive. I promise her I will be safe.

The neighbor lady directly across the road from me is sitting outside. Somjai takes me over to introduce me and explain the situation. They talk quite seriously for a while, the neighbor nodding and eying me. I can infer from the gravity of the conversation that Somjai is conveying the importance of my safety and protection.

Then I learn my luck has continued! My new neighbor, Boontiwa, is an English teacher and speaks English fairly well.

Unusual in rural Thailand, she is a single mother of a teenaged boy and girl. She will become one of my closest friends. I will call her Pi Aw.

The starting offer from Dr. Sombat on rent is so low I'm able to negotiate for….wait for it….an air conditioner! He also arranges for the local water delivery guy to include me on his route. It will cost about a quarter for 10 gallons of potable water. He assures me a rice cooker will be provided. Thai priorities.

Just like that, I have a home. I say goodbye to my friend the bullfrog, and say hello to….lizards.

Thus far I've covered chickens, bugs, dogs, snakes, monkeys and frogs. What I haven't addressed yet is by far the most prolific form of wildlife in Thailand, lizards. Lizards are everywhere in Thailand, inside and out. Specifically, I'm referring to the cute little geckos like the mascot for the Geico commercials. About three to four inches long, they climb the walls and run across the ceiling everywhere. They're a good lizard. They eat insects and avoid humans. At first when I'd see them in my host family's home, they startled me. Now in my new home they are like pets. It's so sad when they mistakenly try to hide in the door frame so that when the door shuts they are sliced in half and die. The good news is if they only get their tail cut off, it grows back!

Very, very, few "indoor" spaces in Thailand are truly indoor. Despite the fact that I have screens on my windows, my front door has just enough space under it to allow geckos in. The bathroom has several 1"X6" openings up high on the wall allowing super easy access to geckos. I will later learn the hard way that if I don't keep a drain strainer over the drainage hole in the middle of my bathroom floor, it is also a passage into my house for critters.

For efficiency, I have the AC mounted on the wall in my bedroom, keeping the door closed at all times. It's nice to lock myself in my comfortably cool bedroom at night, knowing the geckos are busy taking care of insects in other rooms. I feel like they are my little guard dogs (guard lizards?) against the mosquitos.

Every evening I hear the sound of "too-kay! too-kay!" For the longest time, while living with my host family, I assumed they had a cuckoo clock. Every evening at about the same time I'd hear "too-kay!" "too-kay!" Finally some other volunteers cleared up the confusion. It's actually the song of the aptly named tokay lizard. As they are supposed to be good luck, it's comforting to know my house shelters a tokay. Until the day I actually see him in my house.

One day I'm brushing my teeth at my sink when I glimpse movement behind the mirror that's attached to the wall by a mount holding the mirror several inches away from the wall. Slowly I peer behind the mirror and freeze in horror. Unlike the cute little geckos, the tokay is monstrous, as big as my forearm, and scary looking. I had never seen one before because they are notoriously shy. I would be shy too if I was as hideous as that!

Panicked, I run out of my house and yell and motion at a couple of random neighbor guys to come in to my house and help me. They look at me like I am cuckoo-for-cocoa-puffs until I manage to convey the urgency of following me, a total stranger, into my house. When they get to the bathroom and see the problem, they look none too eager to deal with the issue either. But with bat-shit crazy lady jumping up and down and screaming at them, they certainly can't think they have any choice but to help.

They proceed to swat at the tokay and chase him around my bathroom (it's a fairly large room) as I scream bloody murder, "Get him out! "Get him out!" After a few seconds of missteps and dramatic turns that feel like hours to me, they manage to corral him out of the bathroom and out of the house. I breathe a huge sigh of relief, thanking and bowing to the guys who still just look at me like I'm nuts as they go on their way.

There goes MY good luck. Best start feeding the monks again. Might as well grow a few mole hairs just for good measure.

Tokay on my wall.

Chapter 15

The Hot Season

APRIL IN THAILAND is the height of the hot season. Now I am kicking myself for taking a house so far away. Riding home in the 100+ degree temps is miserable. I remind myself Peace Corps is supposed to be hard. But this really, really sucks.

Because it's so hot, April is summer vacation for students in Thailand. Therefore, I haven't started a daily work routine yet. I am still getting my bearings, learning my way around, making myself known in the community, IRBing (Intentional Relationship Building). I'm already tight with Somjai, Mr. Sinit and Principal. I do know now that the Principal's name is Sakun, but since Somjai always calls her "Principal," I just call her "Principal" too. Maybe it's a sign of respect, like "Her Majesty" or "Boss Lady." The four of us are always together. We eat lunch together every day, usually in the principal's air conditioned office, with food we buy from vendors in the market. I understand very little of what's said, but I'm comfortable with my little clique.

We start to make plans about my work in the community. Somjai's first idea is finding scholarship money. Ugh! The dreaded "M" word. It's understandable that money is what they want from the "rich American." The stereotype is that our roads are paved with gold and we're all swimming in cash. While I love the idea of funding needy students, I know my focus must be on sustainable projects, not handing out dollars. I start with what I know best, which is an evening English class for adults in the community. This was suggested by Dr.

Sombat who even provided a room for the class to be held in the hospital. I didn't really come here to be an English teacher, but the community wants what the community wants. Now, what to do with the other 23 hours of my day.

Worried about me being bored during the day, Somjai has an idea. Since her students aren't in school right now, Somjai asks if I want to give an hour long English "activity" one morning at the school. She says it will give me something to do. She arranges everything and tells me when to show up. I prepare some English songs and games to teach the students.

When I finish my hour-long lesson and say goodbye, they all just sit there, staring at me. I go tell the principal in my broken Thai, "I finish teaching. Students no go home."

"They are waiting for their parents to come get them. It's only 10:00," she tells me. "Class is from 9:00 to 12:00."

"Really? It is?" It appears I have misunderstood my task, which will become an all-too-common theme in my life as a volunteer.

"See you tomorrow," she waves me away, seemingly unconcerned if I actually continue my lesson until the finish time or not.

Tomorrow? It turns out my one-hour English "activity" has been promoted as a two-week, three-hour a day English class.

Oooooh-kay. I go back to the classroom, wing some more songs and games for a couple of more hours and vow to lesson plan when I get home. When it finally is time to leave the students all try to give me a bunch of money. I try to refuse the money, but they just leave it on a table. It is strictly forbidden by Peace Corps to accept any money from the Thai people for any work we do. The Peace Corps gives us a modest living allowance that keeps us in equal living standards as our communities. I take this rule very seriously and so take my issue up with the principal. She doesn't care about the rule. She insists that Thai people think if something is free it's no good. So she has to charge or they will think it's a shitty class. Talk about your moral dilemmas. I come up with a solution, the money will go to supplies for the school. I cheat a little bit and buy some candy to give as game prizes to the students.

With the class ending at noon, I'm riding my bicycle home in the heat of the day, in the peak of the hot season, which nearly kills me. The hot air literally burns my lungs as the sun burns my skin even on this short ride home. I know first-hand why hell is depicted as a hot place.

I stop half way home at a local shop for an icy cold Pepsi served in a bag. Yes, I said "in a bag," as in a plastic bag, just big enough to hold eight ounces of Pepsi and some ice. It's really quite brilliant. Since the glass bottles are worth money, and the plastic bags are cheaper than cups, it makes financial sense for the vendors to pour the Pepsi into a bag, keeping the bottle to be refilled. Add in a straw and you're good to go! Like so many things I thought were weird at first, I find this strategy to be brilliant. I will forever swear that Pepsi tastes better in a bag. What I really love is that I can drape the bag handles over my bicycle handle bars and ride away with my Pepsi attached and drink it while I'm riding home. I try NOT to think about the toll on the environment these little plastic bags will take.

Arriving home, I can't wait to douse myself with buckets of cool water standing naked in the middle of my big bathroom floor.

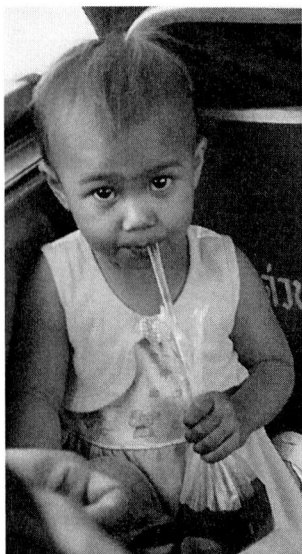
Pepsi sai tung.

If a splash bath isn't heaven when you're boiling hot, I don't know what is. More brilliance on the part of the Thais. The cool-water splash bath vies for greatest invention status along with Pepsi *sai tung* (in a plastic bag).

*   *   *

With April comes the biggest celebration of the year in Thailand.. It's called Songkran and it's celebrated with many prayers and offerings at Buddhist temples. But Sonkgran is really about one huge, week-long water fight. Kids and adults stand on the side of the road with water guns, buckets of water, cups of water, fire hoses…(if it can contain and propel water, it's used during Songkran (and throw water on every human they see). When not throwing water on each other, there's drinking, music and dancing, drinking, food and games, drinking, a parade, drinking, praying at the temple, and then more water fights.

I have asked Somjai why the water fight. She said because it's hot and the water cools people off. Hmmm. It's always hot in Thailand. Water is always cooling. But we have one week for Songkran? There must be more to it.

When interacting with less-than-fluent English speakers, one learns the art of reading between the lines. One learns the art of context. Sleuth-like, one observes closely for clues to the real meaning of what's said. Like a mathematician, we put two and two together, sometimes coming up with five. Or we become a mind reader, literally learn to know what's meant when the words make no sense. At least it seems that way. Hell, sometimes we just guess and hope for the best. This will take some detective work. Keep in mind, this is before the days that Google became a verb and any and all information lies at our fingertips. I bet Google took all the fun out of culture shock!

Initiation into Songkran for me comes the first morning of the celebration as I'm riding my bike into town and some kids along the road run up and throw water on me. Surprise!

I'm on my way to meet Somjai and the rest who are downtown where tables line the streets with massive amounts of donated non-perishable food items. About 50 monks came, and we bow and pray, and they collect all that food and take it home. So we got some good merit, but no one told me to bring a non-perishable food item, and I brought bananas, so I'm not too hopeful about my merit this time.

Next is the parade. I am pretty nervous and excited as I'm slated to carry a banner and lead the parade through town, but that plan changes at the last minute. Somjai breaks the news that I've been de-throned, or de-crowned, if you will. The parade starts at 11:00am which would have me marching all through town in the heat of the day. I'm a little disappointed that I've lost my Queen of the Festival Parade status. I'm ashamed to admit, I always had a secret wish to be the Lilac Queen of my home town's parade, riding on the float, practicing my royal wave for hours in front of the mirror in preparation. But here there is no float. And it's over 100 degrees at 11:00am and the parade march is over an hour long, unshaded. They can't have the farang dying of a heat stroke or passing out mid-parade in front of the whole town after crawling on hands and knees, tongue lolling out like a dog.

Instead, I only have to participate in the dance contest for a while that afternoon. I'm not actually competing, thank god. I'm just being showcased once again. I was a star with my singing, but how will I fare with dancing? Luckily, my Peace Corps pre-service training included beginner lessons and much practice in the art of Thai style dance. I wonder what's next after singing and dancing? A comedy routine? Hell, every day here for me is a comedy routine.

They dress me up in shiny satin blue with frilly lace and layer powder, eye-shadow and lipstick on my face, which seems pointless since I will surely sweat it all off before I even start the dance. They tell me I look like a doll, which I find oddly flattering.

I prance around in the perimeter of the parking lot along with all the other contestants feeling guilty because, of course, all eyes are on me, and what about the dancers who are actually competing? Oh well. The farang can dance Thai style! The crowd goes wild! A star is born again!

I make a few rounds with a smile plastered to my cherry-red painted mouth, getting hotter and hotter, sweatier and sweatier, until I'm given permission to stop. At this point, I run as fast as the heat allows me to the nearest of several fire trucks, its hoses shooting water across the whole lot, and let myself become drenched. I'm so happy I'm ready to do the *"Maniac"* splash-dance from *Flashdance,* feet pounding quickly up and down singing "She's a maniac, maaaaniac on the floor." But I seriously can't handle any exertion. Not to mention it just wouldn't look the same in my frilly, lacey, puffy, blue satin Thai dance costume.

Songkran, as noted above, also involves plenty of rituals for merit, or for as Somjai calls it, "for the good things." With my detective, analysist, mathematician, mindreading skills I determine the meaning "for the good things." Okay, okay, this one is fairly straightforward, especially as it's so inherent to Thai Buddhism. For example, we feed the monks "for the good things." I call it merit. It's really all about good karma. In all selfishness, we want the "good things" to come our way. And who doesn't, really?

So for Songkran, we're back at the temple, bowin' and prayin', prayin' and a bowin'. The last time I was bowing and praying this much I was at a funeral. Although it took me well over an hour to figure out I was even at a funeral. That time we wanted "the good things" for the deceased, and I'm still not really sure who he was. Like a wedding, a funeral is one of those ceremonies that Thais like to drag a farang to.

I'm still sleuthing out the details of what kind of good things we can actually hope for in Thai culture after someone has died. Heaven? A better life once they're reincarnated? I know Thais believe in both. A smooth transition? Don't expect me to figure out these answers from context. Haven't humans been working on this since the beginning of time?

Now that it's Songkran, this time, it's all about me. It's always fun to work towards our own "good things." The volunteer can't help but reflect on altruism and her own "service." We all want to believe that we do good things on their merit alone, because they are the right thing to do as good members of the community or good citizens of the world. But maybe the Thais are on to something with their own transparency.

Farang in Thai dress.

Chapter 16

In Memory of Pi Noi

WAY BACK WHEN, it feels like years ago, but it was barely a few months, I experienced one of the scariest days of my life. I was to be placed with my host family during the two months of training. I was visibly terrified. On that day, I remember early on, as host families were just beginning to arrive, being greeted by a youngish woman, with a friendly, smiling face waving at me. She had two girls with her, about 11 and 12 years old. Once inside the meet and greet room, I glanced at her and she waved at me again, grinning broadly. I found her presence so comforting I hoped she was my host "mother." Of course, she wasn't. But it turns out she was Sara's host mother, living in my training village, very close to where I was going to live.

Their house doubled as a store along that road next to the river, along which we rode our bicycles. The store stocked candy, chips, and pop, stuff neighborhood kids would stop by and purchase with any little spending money they acquired. Even though the house was super rustic compared to my homestay house, I was secretly a little jealous because Sara was told she could help herself to anything in the candy store whenever she wanted. I was also envious because her host mother, Pi Noi, was so darn warm and friendly. As Sara and I were friends, I would often hang out there, accepting offers of free gum or candy. Sometimes Pi Noi would invite all four of us trainees to dinner, where we'd sit on the wood floor with slats looking down to the dirt underneath. In spite of this, it always felt very comfortable to visit there.

We'd been living at our work sites just about three weeks when the tragic news came. Pi Noi had suddenly and unexpectedly died. It was shocking. She was so young and so full of life. I felt for her family, her husband and daughters. I felt for Sara. Of course I would be joining her to attend the funeral. We had become close during our training experience together.

Sara and I traveled from our work sites back to our training site. We met back at our training hotel where we'd planned to stay until after the funeral. Despite the sadness of the occasion, we were happy to see each other again. We'd never gone three weeks without seeing another white person, let alone being able to speak in person with a fellow American. We looked forward to catching up, comparing notes, with maybe a little venting about our hardships. We showered and came down to go grab some dinner when Sara's phone started ringing. It was Pi Chu, one of Sara's old neighbors and Pi Noi's closest friend.

I know this sounds terrible, but per my encouragement, Sara refused to answer her phone. It was quite obvious that someone had seen us arrive in town and had contacted Pi Chu to let her know. The phone rang again. And again. And again. We are not terrible people, we simply wanted a little, tiny break from…Thai-ness. What's harder than the sweltering heat, squat toilets, lizards and bullfrogs, is the social interactions. It's exhausting to put out constant effort to try to speak and understand Thai for any length of time. Even when not on a stage one feels like their constantly putting on a show, holding that required smile on your face endlessly. A break from this performance with a fellow American and friend is fortifying, maybe even necessary for the PCV's survival. At least it was for mine.

Feeling terribly guilty, but not guilty enough to answer the phone, we head out to find a restaurant, only to be followed by the hotel clerk yelling "Telephone!" "Telephone!" in Thai.

We looked at each other in amazement and disbelief. The clever Pi Chu had called the hotel. There was no refusing the call at this time, although I am embarrassed to admit, I briefly considered just continuing walking away pretending we didn't understand what the hotel clerk wanted from us. Never mind she was holding her hand to her ear miming the use of a phone.

Sara took the call, her face dropping as she kept repeating "*kao jai, kao jai.*" (I understand. I understand). She was being blatantly and shamelessly chastised, guilted into having us go stay with Pi Chu instead of at the hotel. Pi Chu wielded the all-powerful "*greng jai*" over our heads like a sword. It's the Thai concept of doing the right thing, thinking of the other person. Literally it translates to "generosity" and is at the heart of Thai culture. In other words, she was saying, "You guys have to come stay with us because we expect it and according to Thai custom it's the right thing to do, and screw your farangness and your selfish foreign ways." At least that's how we interpreted it with our limited Thai. There was no misinterpreting the "I come get you NOW!" in English.

Sara and I looked at each other sadly, sighed, and went back to our room to get out bags.

We couldn't even get our money back because we had already checked in and used the shower. It was only $10.00, but that's a lot of money to a Peace Corps volunteer.

In retrospect it's so obvious that having us stay with them was as much about saving face and their reputation as it was about hospitality, which explains Pi Chu's urgency. How would it look if the farangs chose to stay at a hotel instead of with their Thai friends? Especially for a funeral at which we would be the honored guests. What would the neighbors think? They would think the farangs didn't like their Thai friends. Or worse, found their hospitality wanting. It would bring great shame and embarrassment to Pi Chu.

Pi Chu drove us directly to the temple where we would, per Thai custom, view Pi Noi's body before cremation. On the way, she explained how Pi Noi had died. Apparently Pi Noi went to the doctor because she had been having chest pains. The doctor told her it was just a stomach ache and sent her home. Along the river across from Pi Noi's house is a wooden, shaded, platform where the neighbors congregate to keep cool in the heat of the day. It's a happy, peaceful little hangout where the women socialize and where Pi Noi loved to rest and relax every day. Upon returning from the doctor's visit, Pi Noi went out to the platform to nap in the shade, which was her daily habit. She never woke up. We were told she died of myocardial-infarction. At the time we didn't know what that meant and we didn't have Google to look it up. But given she'd had chest pains we assumed correctly she'd had a heart attack. Not a stomach ache.

Many people were gathered at the temple where Pi Noi's body was in a refrigerated box with windows to peer through. She looked beautiful and peaceful, like she was sleeping. We lit incense, said a prayer, and waited for the monks to lead the evenings chanting for the last night before tomorrow's cremation. I was reminded of the rosary service my Catholic family holds the evening before the funeral and burial, except we sat on the floor and the chanting was Sanskrit, not Latin.

Back at Pi Chu's we readied for sleep. She had prepared mats for us on her bedroom floor. We would all be sleeping in the same room, Thai-style. The room was big enough for only her bed and two mats on the floor. Sara and I would sleep on the mats. Pi Chu and her 10 year old daughter would sleep on the bed. She said her husband and son were gone. She kept joking about snoring, which was no joke because I kept waking to loud snoring in the middle of the night, snoring that sounded oddly masculine.

Early in the morning, when Sara and I started to stir, from the bed we're greeted loudly by a man's voice in Thai, "Good morning!" Sara and I burst out laughing. Then we hear the 13 year old son, "Good morning!" More laughing. We'd had no idea that all six of us had slept in the room that night, four of them in the bed together. And Pi Chu wondered why we wanted to stay at the hotel!

At noon we went back to the temple again to eat and pray, even though the funeral wasn't until 3:00. More waiting. More praying.

Pi Noi's 20 year old brother-in-law became a monk for a couple of days "for the good things" for Pi Noi (Yes, one can take an emergency monkhood status as needed). While we were inside the temple praying, he was outside having his head shaved and being draped in orange robes.

For the funeral ceremony, Pi Noi had been moved from the refrigerated box into a regular coffin that was also transparent. A procession was led by Pi Noi's oldest daughter, 13, carrying incense. She was remarkably graceful and dignified. She was followed by her 11-year-old sister carrying a large framed photo of her mother, just as graceful, smiling bravely. Next came the husband, looking exhausted, followed by about 20 monks with a big decorated cart escorted by family members. This procession circled the temple three times, then placed the coffin up on a table. Each funeral attendee was given a paper flower to place next to the coffin and was given a bar of soap to take with them. I have no idea what the soap was for, but probably something to do with "the good things."

Then the box was opened and people rushed to have one last look at Pi Noi's body. I wasn't tall enough to see over the edge but Mark could, and he said she didn't look like Pi Noi at all. I guess she had already started to change since being removed from refrigeration.

Someone cut open a coconut and sprinkled milk over her body and all the paper flowers were put in the box as well as a blue fluid that I'm assuming was flammable. With everyone standing right there, they put the body into the cement incinerator and ignited it, shutting the incinerator. This was too much for Mark and he pulled me away roughly.

Funerals are supposed to be happy occasions in Thailand, and crying isn't common. But oh, how people cried at Pi Noi's funeral. I was glad to see them grieving for her, a devout Buddhist, a loving mom, a kind friend who will be dearly missed. I decided I like the Buddhist concept that with all our prayers and offerings and from Pi Noi's own countless kind and good deeds, that whatever her afterlife holds, she would receive the merit of "the good things." She certainly deserved them.

Chapter 17

Fun with Bad Dog

SOMJAI IS AMAZING. She works her butt off. She looks after me. And she's always trying to improve her English, which is oh so much more than I can say for me and learning Thai. She often asks me questions about English phrases and vocabulary. It's given me some real perspective on language acquisition.

One day she asked me about a word she'd heard in a movie.

"Amy, what is this dogson? Many times I hear 'dogson' in a movie."

Dogson? Dogson? What the hell is she talking about?

Then it dawns on me. She has made a literal translation from "son of a bitch." Oh my.

"It's very impolite," I explain. "People say it when you are mad or call someone you really don't like. Please never ever say it."

"But what does it mean?" ever the learner, Somjai persists.

"Never mind. Just don't say it."

Then she asks, "What about this 'fuck you' I'm always hearing in the movies?"

More than a little shocked, I tell Somjai "fuck you" is probably the worst of all the impolite language in English and please, please never, ever say it.

"Then why do I always hear it in the movies?"

Sigh. Any parent out there knows what language a child picks up on first. Something about the emotion behind these phrases, not to mention the repetition, that makes them stand out and easy to remember. It's not uncommon for us volunteers to hear children call out to us as we're riding our bicycles, "Fuck you! Fuck you!" They have no idea what it means. They simply want to say something to us in English, and that's what they know in English. Thank you Hollywood.

Then there are some words and phrases in English that just sound funny to Thai people. Kind of like "*ba ba bo bo*" sounds funny to English speakers. As an English teacher to second language speakers, you get used to students laughing unpredictably to some new word or phrase. Take this example:

The school has a dog. It's not one of those scabby, mangy, hairless types, but a cute fluffy chow chow, who must be hotter than hell living in this climate.

Chow chows like to nip. It's just what they do.

One day during the break I rode my bicycle in to the school, arriving in the principal's office panting and sweaty and red-faced.

"What's the problem?" asks Principal. "It's only a ten minute ride." Touche. In other words, we told you not to take a house so far away from the school, dumbass farang.

I sit down on the couch and give the dog a pat when he starts nipping at my hand.

"Bad dog," I gently scold him.

Principal starts laughing like crazy. "Bad. Dog," she repeats, in her halting English, laughing even harder. By the way she was laughing, it was the most hilarious thing she'd ever heard. She goes around all day for the next several months saying "bad dog." Sometimes we change it to "good dog," with the same response of hilarity. We will end up getting a lot of mileage out of "bad dog," but I never will understand why it's so damn funny to Principal. I think it might just sound really funny to her.

Mr. Sinit is the youngest in our clique, the only male, and is often the brunt of our jokes. One day, Somjai was at her favorite past time of teasing Mr. Sinit, and she kept hitting him, over and over. Fed up, Mr. Sinit actually grabbed her arm mid-strike, reached out his mouth and bit it! (The reader knows what's coming, right?) "Bad dog!" Poor Mr. Sinit. No one likes to be the bad dog, but that is his new nickname. As a former monk, he's a good sport.

Another time we were at yet another one of those events where I have to sing on a stage in front of 100 people and they present flowers to me. Then a bunch of other "official" types join me on the stage in a line as the mayor places a garland of fresh flowers around each of our necks. Later, the principal asks me what we call this garland in English. For the life of me, at the time, I cannot remember the word "garland." I can only think of the word "lei," perhaps because I took a trip to Hawaii right before coming to Thailand. I explain that they are not common on the mainland US, but are very popular in Hawaii. She gestures to the dog in front of us, holding up her garland in an outward gesture and says, "I'm going to lay (lei) the bad dog." Who's laughing her ass off now? This volunteer. I almost fall off my chair. At the same time, I'm a tiny bit impressed with her ability to use the noun "lei" like a verb in that way.

Chapter 18

Indiana Jo[4] and the Temple of Bat Doo

WE'RE IN THE MIDDLE OF SUMMER VACATION for students all over Thailand when Principal invited me on her summer family trip. Where would it be? An amusement park? A water park? A beach? No kids, we're spending our summer trip in a dark, dank, stinky, spider infested, bat infested, bat poop infested cave. Did I mention we will sit in said cave and meditate until we reach spiritual enlightenment?

Since it's still my policy to accept all invitations, and since I'm still naïve enough not to know what an invitation to go meditate in a cave entails, I agree to go. I'm learning that Principal and her family are quite the devout Buddhists, hence going on a meditation retreat for their summer vacation. I equate it with Christians sending their kids to Bible Camp in the summer. I know Christians do meditation retreats as well, but I don't think of those as family trips.

Principal and her family speak very little English. Luckily, Principal has a talking dick, I mean, talking *dict,* which is the Thai word for dictionary. She relies heavily on her talking dict to communicate with me. I actually think we have more communication problems using the talking dict than not because the translations are so wonky. For example, when she wanted to ask me what my religion was, thanks to her best friend the

---

4 My middle name is Jo. I have friends who actually call me Jo. In case there are readers young enough not to know the movie, this is a reference to the very famous Harrison Ford "Indiana Jones and the Temple of Doom" movie from the 80s. If you haven't seen it, you should!

talking dict, she asked instead "Who do you hold in esteem? Who do you respect?" I started to tell her that I held her in esteem, that I respected her. But we both gathered right away that I wasn't implying I worshipped her as a god.

Actually, that's a very common question for me here. People are always asking me the question about my religion and I never know how to answer it. I've started telling people that I am many religions, Buddhist, Christian, Jewish, Muslim, Hindu, etc. That's not going over so well. They look at me like I'm crazy, obviously assuming I've misunderstood the question. Sometimes it's safest to leave it at that, a misunderstanding, since it's most often the truth anyways.

I was actually really excited to learn more about Buddhism by living in Thailand. What little I'd gleaned from my personal studies resonated with me. Unfortunately however, mostly what I'm learning here is how to bow and light incense, feed the monks, and ask for the good things. I could save myself a lot of grief if I'd practice the Buddhist teachings that I do know about from earlier studies. Life is suffering. Every moment is fleeting. Non-attachment. "This, too, shall pass."

Every time I've tried to embrace these teachings in my daily life I've become frustrated and given up immediately. It's too hard. The same for meditation. Too difficult. So boring to sit and pay attention to my breathing. Impossible to quiet the "monkey mind." Maybe a meditation retreat to the caves is just what I need.

On the ride to the caves it becomes apparent that Principal assumes I don't know what meditation is so she pulls out her handy dandy talking dict. I humor her by reading on the screen what the definition is for meditation. "To stare at the breath." Electronic dictionaries are notorious for giving strangely literal meanings for some words. But I like this. It seems oddly accurate.

When we arrive at the caves we first go over to the temple where a monk is sitting on the floor next to some burning incense. I'm introduced and Principal hands over 1000 baht, ($25) which is a good chunk of change for Thai people and surely "for the good things." We all sit together and they chat. It seems like Principal is telling him about me, as he keeps smiling at me kindly and nodding. I'm secretly hoping to get in on some of the "good things" even though I didn't give him any money.

Finally we enter one of the caves. I've never been in a real cave before. Of course I've seen the famous images from Lascaux where our ancestors invented art. But really when I think of a cave, in my mind I see this rather shallow indentation into a mountainside, maybe tall enough to stand up in, probably big enough to build a fire to sleep around, but just barely. So I am shocked to see that once we crept through an opening barely big enough to fit our bodies through, especially my fat farang body, the cave was at least 75 feet tall and maybe miles deep. The monks who maintain the caves have electricity connected inside to power light fixtures, but those were few and far between. Mostly we have to rely on the measly rays of light we could muster out of our pathetic little flashlights. I managed to squeeze out just enough light to reveal the hundreds of bats blanketing the ceiling and walls of the cave and the inches deep bat feces embedded on the floor. And if I shined the light in the exact right place I could see the hugest spiders that I had ever seen in my life. I'm not even afraid of spiders, but when I pointed out one on the cave wall to the principal's daughter and she generously flicked it out of the way, right into my hair, even I had to scream. This is where we had come to meditate?

When meditation is supposed to be working with the breath, "staring at the breath," why on earth would you go into a stinky, musty, moldy, cave to poison yourself with toxins from bat poop while taking in all that breath? What with the smell and other distractions I was hugely unsuccessful at mastering any peace of mind. I was completely unable to even stare at my breath.

After the first in-cave meditation session the daughters took me exploring into several other caves and I discovered more pleasant and aesthetic aspects. It felt ancient and mythical being deep inside the earth like this, and sometimes the walls were sparkly and beautiful. Often we'd find statues of Buddha and other shrines and altars throughout the caves. I never quite understand the connection between caves and Buddhism. Apparently some monks are like the aesthetics of old and hang out in these caves seeking enlightenment.

When I head towards one of the caves to explore, Principal's daughter holds back and tells me no. She won't let me go into this particular cave.

"Why?" I ask.

She said this one has a goat in it and she was afraid.

"A goat?" I ask, befuddled.

"A goat!" she insists, adamant I should not enter this cave.

What the heck? She flung a freaking spider at me! Now she's afraid of a goat?

"Very scary. A goat. You know? Dead?!" she explains.

"Oh! A GHOST!" Now I'm afraid to go into that one too. It was enough to deal with the bats and spiders and other creepy crawlies of the cave without contending with a ghost as well.

After dinner we prayed and chanted for a couple of hours. Then Principal, her daughters and I went to "bed" on a row of thin mats on the living room floor of the nuns' house. The lights were turned out at 9:00 p.m., and I tried to fall asleep. This was a challenge not only because the floor was cement and my mat was so thin, but also because ten or so of the other guests were still milling about and talking in voices set at a very high volume. Note to self: Apparently it is not considered impolite by Thais to be very loud in a room where others are trying to sleep. In fact, I am learning that Thai people have a gift for sleeping through just about anything, therefore they find no need to respect others' sleep. Case in point, take the Thai bus ride. As sure as the sun will rise in the morning, a Thai bus will be blaring music as loud as possible. Just as surely, Thai people on the bus will be fast asleep. So I'm not exactly surprised that Principal and her daughters are soon snoring away, while hours later, the loud ladies chatting away, I'm wide awake pondering the meaning of the life and questioning my decision to join the Peace Corps, when I could be sleeping soundly in a comfortable bed in a quiet room, by myself, or at least not with 20-some strangers.

Hours later, when it did finally quiet down, I managed to fall asleep, only to wake every time I tried to roll over on the hard ground. So when someone started clanging the prayer bell loudly and I looked at my watch and it said 3:00 a.m. I was sure my watch had stopped. But no, it was really 3:00 a.m. I thought, you have got to be kidding me and no way am I getting up to pray. I'd done enough praying for the day, even though it was technically the next day. For me that was enough praying for the month. Then I noticed that Principal and her daughters were not getting up. In fact, still snoring away, they didn't even appear to notice the obnoxiously loud and still clanging bell. Phew! Soon the bell would stop and I could go back to sleep. Alas, no sooner had the bell stopped than the monks started up with the chanting. Into a microphone. Over the loudspeaker.

For the love of god! (Literally). Can a woman please get just a little rest? This is our vacation, for god's sake. (Literally). I started asking myself how long this could last and thought two hours easily. Imagine my surprise when I found that I had actually gone back to sleep until 5:00 a.m. when everyone woke and started to stir. Maybe I'm starting to adapt after all.

Here's the fascinating thing about Thai monks. Some of them are surely Hell's Angels recruits. Think of this image. Young men with heads shaved bald. They are frequently tattooed as part of being a monk. Sometimes they are missing teeth, because dental care in Thailand is questionable. Some smoke cigarettes. And they ride motorcycles! If they just traded the orange robes for leather, Hell's Angels for sure. No wonder I find them so attractive.

Chapter 19

Green Pudding Sandwiches in the Rain

THE TIMES THEY ARE A CHANGIN'! The modern world is coming to Thailand. I read it in the newspaper. A 25-year-old law requiring boys in school to wear crew cuts has been overturned. This is big, people. Huge. This law had been taken very seriously. I witnessed it myself, when one boy whose parents neglectfully let his hair start to get a little fuzzy on the sides was drug into the cafeteria to have some teacher go at his head with the clippers. No joke. In the cafeteria. Which is outside. And which they call "the canteen." The one exception was the one little boy who had a 24 inch long braid sprouting from a small patch on the top of his head. They did keep the rest of his head shaved. What's next? No uniforms? Choosing what to wear to school? It could happen. Surely society will become illiterate at that point.

And all the letters to the editor! Education is going to hell in a hand basket! Boys MUST wear their hair in crew cuts! Otherwise, they will be so focused on their hair they won't pay attention to their studies. All this time, back in the US, I thought I was just a boring teacher. Really, it was the hair. The boys were just too focused on their hair to be successful in my high school English class. Therefore, I think I can solve all of the problems with the American education system. Require buzz cuts for boys! Surely they can't be learning anything if they are choosing their own style of hair.

Now, the students in my adult English class are absolutely allowed to choose their own hair style, but they do have an interesting list of rules to follow. Here's how the rules transpired.

I approached my principal with the proposition of an adult English class at the school because so many adults in the community have expressed an interest in learning English. In my mind, we could start getting the word out, gather up 20 or so interested students, and I'd start teaching in a couple of weeks. I was thinking I'd have an hour long class one night a week. She proposed three hours a night, every night of the week. With skilled negotiation I was able to talk her down to two hours on Tuesdays and Thursdays. She talked me into starting this week.

"And by the way, we want a typed up syllabus with objectives for each class, for the whole 40 hour class."

"Oh, and you need to make a list of class expectations because Thai people are not good about being on time and will skip class."

I laughed out loud. I told her point blank I didn't care if they didn't come to class. They are adults and can choose for themselves whether to come to class or not. I wanted to teach students who wanted to learn. They are responsible for their own learning.

"So you won't make the list of expectations?" she asks.

"Nope."

"Okay, then I will make it for you. What do you want it to say?" she asks.

"I don't want it to say anything!" I've lost my patience yet again. "If you're making it, you decide what it should say."

It turns out that for my English class:

- You MUST be 20-years-old to attend.
- You MUST arrive no later than five minutes after class starts.
- If you are absent more than once you will not receive a certificate of completion.

This last one is the worst threat of all. Thai people take their certificates very seriously. No wonder only three people showed up the first night, including the principal and her daughter who were 10 minutes late!

Rumor has it that 15 people from "the office" told the principal they would be attending my class. However, they were then told by my supervisor that I would get into trouble and be sent away if they came. Actually, it IS true that I would be sent away. That is, IF I accepted the 800 baht that the principal wanted to charge each student, after I explicitly insisted that she not.

So it kind of warms my heart that they didn't show up. If they had shown up, that would mean they wanted me to get sent away. I take it as a very nice compliment that they stayed away. What does not warm my heart is the rest of the rumor that actually the reason the supervisor told the office workers this was to sabotage the principal's plan because he is jealous that I am not working with him more. What, pray tell, am I supposed to do with him? I've never heard him speak one lick of English? And what is this anyway? Junior high school?

The second class had seven people, including the principal, this time 15 minutes late. There goes her certificate! I reprimanded her as a "bad dog" and she swears she will be on time to the next class.

I've always believed that teaching is about learning. Here is what I'm learning from teaching my adult English class.

1) I have a funny accent. When I listen to my students try to mimic my pronunciation of some words, it sounds awfully nasal.

2) Maybe I'm the wrong person to teach English pronunciation.

3) It is more rewarding to teach students who actually want to learn what you are teaching.

4) It's much easier to teach when you are provided a curriculum. It's much harder to pull everything you teach out of thin air.

5) Therefore, Principal's requirement of coming up with all the learning objectives in advance was a solid idea.

Slowly, I'm developing relationships outside my little school clique of Somjai, Principal and Bad Dog. For example, I have a new friend from my class. She is a tiny, jolly woman who is the giggliest gal I've ever seen. Her name is Dick, which makes me giggly. She insists on driving me home from class every night. Despite the fact that I have a light on my bicycle, no one wants me to ride my bicycle home after class in the dark.

She also brings me treats every night. Usually green pudding sandwiches. Actually, I have no idea what's between the bread but it's creamy, green and tastes like coconut pudding. I'm not sure if I don't like the taste of green pudding sandwiches or if I can't get past the color.

In all fairness, Thai people find a lot of farang food disgusting, too. Take butter. What's better than butter? Nothing. But when I try to get Somjai to taste peanut butter, she refuses, insisting it must have butter in it, and she hates the taste of butter. This frustrates me to no end, because anyone who's eaten Thai food knows that a lot of it tastes like peanut butter, because they use peanuts and coconut milk, a combination that tastes just like peanut butter, at least to me. After a bunch of pleading and cajoling, and then making her read the list of ingredients on the jar, I finally convince Somjai to taste peanut butter. She loved it. In fact, she insists we can make it ourselves instead of my paying a pretty penny for it in the international section of the supermarket in Korat. Of course she's right. We're always pulling out the mortar and pestle she keeps in her classroom to "bok bok" our favorite green papaya salad. If we "bok bok" the peanuts long enough, we're going to end up with peanut butter. That will save me a lot of money, because I've created a monster. Somjai can't get enough of the stuff. I think she might actually be addicted to peanut butter sandwiches. Which, even she will agree, are much better than green pudding sandwiches.

* * *

Now it's the rainy, or monsoon season. A monsoon is something that I had to experience before I would truly understand its meaning. Thai rainstorms are incredible. I've never experienced anything like it, even living on the East Coast of the US. I've never heard thunder so loud or seen so much water fall from the sky at one time. "Coming down in sheets" has a whole new meaning for me. The world becomes immediately immersed in water. Roads flood instantly. There will be no riding my bicycle in this rain even if they let me.

Much to my chagrin, the rains bring the frogs. One was jumping around my classroom distressing me immensely to the delight of my students. On the ride home that night, my giggling chauffeur points out the people with flashlights meandering in the ditches alongside the road.

"What are they doing?" I ask.

"Looking for frogs," she says. Then after a dramatic pause, "To eat!" as she bursts into another fit of giggles.

The next day when the sun comes out and dries up the world, my road to work looks like a war zone for frogs that are lying all over the road dead and mashed up from being run over by cars in the night. I ride my bicycle slowly, dodging the casualties. I stop and cross myself, an unconscious habit left over from my Catholic girlhood. I'm hoping for the "good things" for the deceased souls. I'm not sure why I assume the frogs have souls. I sigh, realizing it was hopeless for these little monsoon warriors. It was either the highway or a restaurant kitchen chopping board.

Chapter 20

Bureaucracy and Broken Faces

Letter to sister: Thank you for the package!
Especially the chocolate and books! The chocolate
was a little melted but still satisfying. Am I happy?
Occasionally. The last couple of weeks, not at all.
Today, better. But I didn't embark on this adventure for
happiness, or pleasure, or fun. So is it what I expected?
Yes and no. I expected it to be hard and unpleasant,
but in different ways. I hoped that I would learn from
the experience and grow as a person, but that is left
to be seen. I regularly have to talk myself into staying
here. And I haven't even started the real "work" of my
volunteer service yet. Patience is the key, and has never
been one of my stronger attributes. I keep trying.
Give my love to everyone, Amy

HAVE I MENTIONED that it's hot in Thailand? While in some
ways I think I'm getting used to the heat, or at least have
learned how to ignore it, sometimes it's downright miserable.
Especially when the power goes out and I temporarily have no
AC or fan. I get religion real fast and start praying to god for
mercy and lord, please let there be power. This is one of my
only complaints about my home. That, and every morning
I have no running water. It seems that every person in the
neighborhood and their dogs are using the running water
at the same time, making it nonexistent in my house. That's
really a non-issue what with the big vat of water and plastic

buckets in the bathroom. That's how I have to flush my toilet anyway, with or without running water. But since I was complaining…

It's not the heat, however, that makes life hard. It's not even the humidity. It's not the squat toilets, frogs, lizards, or the language barrier. (Okay, sometimes it IS the language barrier). It's not the bus that won't stop for you, even though you are sitting at the bus stop bench at 6:00 in the morning. (The bus won't stop because you haven't stood up and waved in the middle the road. And you can't just wave. They will think you are just being friendly. You must gesture to stop with the palm facing down.) One day, two busses passed me up before the principal came and picked me up, forgetting to tell me that she had planned to pick me up anyway. While these are all challenging, they're not what's hardest for me. It's not even being asked by Somjai every day if I have bathed.

What is much worse for me as a PCV, is the red tape here that gives a whole new meaning to the phrase "bureaucratic bullshit." Thai bureaucracy, combined with power-tripping and the desperate need to "save face," are the bane of my existence. These are driving me crazy, pushing me to my absolute limits and just might push me over the edge.

First there is the Thai obsession with paperwork. One can't pass gas in this country without filing an extensive, hand-written report documenting the details of it. Computers are everywhere here, but the reports are always handwritten. In this vein, Somjai tells me to save every lesson plan, every piece of student work submitted, every piece of used toilet paper, to use for "a presentation" later. I'm kidding about the toilet paper, but it feels that way. By the way, as an experienced teacher, most of my lesson plans are right up here. (Insert visual of me tapping my temple with my index finger).

Then there is this Thai thing about social status. Thai society divides itself into a stratified hierarchy of rank, where the highest person receives the most respect. I've already touched on this a little with the "pi-nong" system, where age is one of the factors of rank. But age is much less a factor in one's social standing than one's job, education and income. With rank comes not only respect, but power. With power, comes power-tripping, especially from the mid-level management who are frustrated with what little power they have, therefore wielding it like a sword.

At the time, I was naïve, and still unconscious of the realities of class in my own country. While I knew inequality was a shameful reality regarding race in the US, I had been innocently sheltered from the reality of class differences among white people. I would later become much more enlightened, but at the time, I was blissfully unaware. Furthermore, I come from the field of education, which is very different culture from the corporate world. Later, when I return to the US and make a brief foray into the corporate world I will learn that hierarchy and power tripping is alive and well in the US as well.

At the time however, I still believed I was from a country based on equality. Self-righteous and as naïve as I was, I didn't think because someone had a better job, or made more money, or was better educated, this made them higher than me. Thai people do. At the same time, I was also unconscious of feeling myself higher-classed than others if I was better educated or made more money (as if!). Therefore, I was caught off guard when I encountered this attitude in Thailand. It literally put the "shock" into culture shock for me.

Hand-in-hand with Thai hierarchy is the Thai people's desperate need to save face. I get it. No one likes to feel embarrassed. The words for "lose face" in Thai language mean literally "broken face." Who wants a broken face? Americans have their own subtle ways of face-saving as well. The little white lies or excuses we make if we make a mistake or forget something important. Thai culture takes it to a new level.

Bureaucracy, along with Thais' value of power and prestige while needing to save face combine to create a perfect storm of mayhem and misery in my life.

Take this case in point. One day I needed to go to "the office" to get a signature. "The office" is in the town's municipal building where people like the superintendent of schools, and other official, self-important people who don't seem to have much work to do, go every day. All PCVs are supposed to spend some time one day a week at "the office." Supposedly, this is where we connect with the community, learn its needs, network, hobnob, and I don't really know what. Turns out, most PCVs just read their mail and write a letter or two. Remember the Seinfeld episode where George goes to his office at Yankee stadium but literally has zero work to do?

Since no one at my office speaks English, and my Thai is still pretty much limited to "I like pineapple," I could see little point in spending time there. What were we going to say to each other? Share a laugh over our love of pineapple?

But alas, on this particular day, as a mere formality, an all too common and crazy-making formality, I required a signature from my supervisor. I approach this situation with an inherent bias. I hate wasting paper. I despise wasting time. I disdain formalities such as getting a signature for the sake of having a signature. Is the task at hand necessary? It is? Great! Fine! I'm happy to comply. But if I can't see a good reason for making an extra effort or wasting someone's time, I'm less than willing.

Trying to be a good sport, I humor myself, perhaps this signature really is necessary. I know I need it to get reimbursed by Peace Corps for rent money. What my supervisor has to do with it is beyond me. But just maybe there's a really good reason my supervisor needs to sign the form that had my address and the cost of my rent. Never mind that I had already sent this information with a receipt including my landlord's signature. But I'm skeptical. Another piece of paper. Another signature. Another trip to the post office.

Upon arriving at the office I ask my supervisor to please sign the form, which is crystal clear, written in Thai and English. It should take less than 10 seconds to slap that old John Hancock on there. I even know the word for signature in Thai. This is not a complicated situation. Or so I thought. He starts looking at the paper with concern. He's hemming and hawing and rubbing his jaw with his eyebrows all furrowed. He shuffles through a bunch of papers. Stacks and stacks of papers. I go sit down. This is obviously more than a 10-second signature procedure. I wait a while.

Then I'm directed to another big shot's office. I actually like this big shot. He's the one who picked me up at the bus station the first day and said I'm not farang, but *khon Thai.* He's amiable and funny. But when he gets that paper in his hands that I needed signed, he now starts rubbing his jaw and hemming and hawing and shuffling through papers.

Ten, maybe 15 minutes have passed and I just want the damn signature. I feel like I'm in an episode of Saturday Night Live and I'm the one normal person who can't understand what's going on with the others. I very politely request in Thai that he please sign it so I can get it in the mail.

"No."

"No?" I ask in disbelief. Then a bunch of Thai language that I don't understand.

He makes a phone call and I watch in disbelief as he starts yelling angrily into the phone. The only word I understand is my name. What the hell? This is not good.

Then my phone rings. It's the principal. Where is Somjai, she wants to know. Somjai is the only one of these people who speaks any kind of passable English and they need her to translate. No one can reach Somjai. I actually just left Somjai. I happen to know that the battery on her phone is dead.

Finally, the papers they've been looking for have been found. It happens to be the report from the conference in Bangkok where we met with our Thai counterparts to learn about working together. This is the conference my supervisor was supposed to have attended so he would know what I was doing in his district. He did not attend. He sent Somjai in his stead. My educated guess is that he was ashamed of his inability to speak English and was afraid to lose face at the conference, so he sent the best English speaker to do his dirty work.

Of course, Somjai is the one who wrote the report about the conference. In fact, she is the one who got yelled at for not getting it to my supervisor on time. Why didn't the ever-reliable Somjai get the report in on time? Because the other teacher from a different school was supposed to sign it and get her principal's signature. However, because the other teacher was fighting with her principal, she didn't get that signature. Therefore, she didn't get the report to the office, getting Somjai in trouble.

It is at this very moment while I'm waiting, waiting, and still waiting for that freaking signature that my supervisor decides to actually read the report Somjai wrote about what I'm doing as a volunteer in his district. Enter Somjai, looking very shy and frustrated, sneaking me a roll of the eyes. She answers a few questions timidly. The supervisor then picks up the phone and calls the goddamn Peace Corps office in Bangkok!

Why is he so reluctant to sign it? I want to cry. Please, please just sign it. I ask Somjai quietly why he won't sign it. Hiding her irritation from him but not from me she tells me that he hasn't read her report so he doesn't know what the paper is that he's supposed to sign. Shit, I sign things all the time that I haven't read. What's the big deal?

A few minutes later he's off the phone, all smiles, and signs the form. I've been sitting there almost an hour.

It's something like this all the time.

I know I have an issue with patience. I have no doubt it's very good for me to be forced to learn patience. I will learn patience. But I will not learn to appreciate bureaucracy and I will not learn to accept waste. I refuse. I'm sorry I can't embrace Buddha's wisdom and all the dharma about non-judgement. Buddha never had to deal with Thai bureaucracy.

It's all the more confusing and crazy-making because it contradicts everything I've been taught about Thai culture. Thai people are supposedly easy-going, laid back, chill. I have witnessed they do have a more lax approach to work. I was taught Thais place great value on harmony and will go to great lengths to avoid conflict. Thai language is full of terms expressing these ideas. Thais value *jai yen*, or "cool heart." There's no need to get angry. The most common phrase in Thai language is *mai pen rai*. It means "never mind" or "it doesn't matter" or "let it go." After what I've just witnessed, *mai pen rai* my ass.

So no. It's not the heat. It's not the humidity. It's all this instead that has the potential to drive me absolutely, certifiably, bonkers, cuckoo, insane in the membrane.

At the same time, while there are a million things here about which to be miserable, there's also something quite delightful in showing up at "the office" at 9:00 in the morning and being offered a cold beer or a wine cooler. It's wonderfully heartwarming to come home from work every day and be greeted by my 10-year-old neighbor "A" (pronounced as the short "a" sound, as in apple) running up to me and giving me a huge hug every time she sees me. There's something so lovely about eating at the neighborhood patio food stand, where the lady serves me extra-large portions for a discounted price because "I look nice." Even better is when I get the whole meal for free because the local policemen happen to be eating there too and insist on paying for mine. Thai hospitality rocks, I tell you. And one final confession about what makes my life here so pleasant, so good. I am embarrassed to admit this because it feels like a PCV fail, but here it is. I don't have to do my own laundry. Laundry service is included in my rental agreement. Bureaucracy, broken-faces, and other frustrations be damned. *Mai pen rai. Jai yen.*

Life is good.

Chapter 21

When Martha Stewart Meets Rural Thailand

May 12, Mass Email to Friends and Family

Well, folks, it's been a rough go lately. Of course, I expected a challenge, and knew there would be times of loneliness and frustration. But still… But still. Now I'm feeling a bit better and so can muster the energy to pound out a few words on these keys and re-establish contact with my life back home. Last Friday was just a really, really tough day emotionally. It's a good thing I'm not close to an airport. I would have jumped on a plane and come home.

I'VE BEEN INVITED on one last outing before school starts. I wasn't actually invited. Somjai called me up and said she'd be coming by later to pick me up to take me to her farm. I got off the phone and started to cry. I'd had a rough week. I wanted to have some alone time to gather up my strength. I have been putting off this visit to Somjai's farm since my first week here. She goes there every weekend. All I really know is that this is a noni farm. Noni is a fruit that is supposed to have some healing or regenerative properties. Her family is growing it to make some tincture or drink that they can market to the health conscious.

So why do I dread this visit to her farm so much? With all due respect to Somjai, her house on Teacher Row, like all of the teachers' houses, is what I call rustic. Very rustic, even by Thai standards. I'm thinking, if her house is this rustic, what will the farm be like? Because I've heard few details, my imagination goes wild. The way she refers to it as "her" farm, I'm assuming it's a family farm, like maybe she grew up there or something. I'm imagining corrugated tin walls and roof, hot as can be, 10 of us sleeping on the floor under a mosquito net. I imagine a concrete "bathroom" infested with all kinds of spiders, frogs, and who knows what else. I'm thinking mud, and cow poop and chickens everywhere.

But Somjai has been so very good to me and I know it means a lot to her for me to visit the farm. So after a very long cry, I wipe my tears, blow my nose, and pack my bag.

A funny thing happened on the way to the farm. The scenery started to get really beautiful. Where we live, the land is flat, dry, and brown. One sees few trees or green anywhere. Now, looking out the windows I see lush, green rolling hills. I'm reminded a little of Hawaii. I'd forgotten that parts of Thailand are considered very beautiful, as I'm living somewhere, well…not. Seeing all these shades of green and beautiful scenery makes me so happy, it almost breaks open my heart.

Even as we passed ramshackle corrugated tin houses and I thought, "oh god, oh god, here we go," it was still okay. I told myself, "I can do this." Surely the conditions can't be worse than anything I've already endured. And at least the surroundings are lovely.

A funnier thing happened when we got to the farm. I literally had to blink my eyes hard, shake my head, and do a double and triple take. It looked like we were driving up to a beach resort, minus the beach, with a man-made pond instead. What I see before me is impeccably landscaped, adorable, open-aired, bungalows on a hillside overlooking a pond with a view of green mountains beyond. On the hills behind the bungalows are noni fields, as far as the eye can see.

As we arrive and park the truck, out walks the most beautiful Thai woman I have ever seen. She's greeting me in fluent English! Maybe I am dreaming! She tells me how happy she is to finally meet me after hearing so much about me. Suddenly I become very self-conscious in the presence of this woman who looks like a movie-star. I am in my Peace Corps casuals, looking like a frumpy American slob. I've just met "Madame."[5] She is Somjai's sister. I start to realize this is actually her farm. Well, her American husband's farm. I realize this is going to be an interesting weekend.

Madame welcomes me into the kitchen, which is a huge open space covered with an island resort style grass roof. It's dusk, so candles are glowing everywhere. A shining teak wood bar includes a stereo and huge speakers. All of this exotic decor overlooks the pond and the mountains and the landscaped yard with flowers of purple and yellow everywhere.

Somjai introduces me to a woman in the kitchen who is preparing food.

"Amy, this is my housewife." The rest of the weekend she refers to her as the maid, so I think her sister corrected her. Housekeeper. Housewife. I didn't care. I just wished I had one.

I'm also introduced to Pa, who's working on his nightly whiskey routine, and Ma, who is making her way to the little house next to the kitchen. It's the parent's house, built specifically for them this year and built even before the main house, which is yet to be built. Everything else was built just this year. They just acquired the farm this year. All this, adding to the beach house in Hawaii, the house in Vegas, and the ski house in Sun Valley, where, Madame discreetly informs me, she has met Demi Moore and other movie stars. Of course they also have an apartment in Bangkok.

5 Ironically, in my next life, when I am married to a man from another country, I am also referred to by everyone in his family as "Madame." It's a thing.

I'm absolutely dying to meet the American husband. I haven't seen another farang in weeks. The only thing I know about him is that he's a 60-year-old ex-Marine, married to a 38-year-old Thai beauty. Unfortunately, he's not at the farm this weekend. They promise I'll meet him another time. And that he owns a lot of houses.

Madame then takes me on a tour of the farm, which I now insist we call an orchard or a plantation. We pass the spirit houses up on the hill, which are nicer than most houses Thai people live in. The sisters bow, and I'm expected to as well, so I do. Madame informs me there is powerful magic here. It's so beautiful up on the hill overlooking the noni trees and the pond and the mountains, I think I know what she means by magic. We're standing on the spot where the main house, her house, is to be built, including a swimming pool. The house is to be open-aired, or Bali style, as Madame describes the style she prefers to live in. She relays to me that her husband says to her when they stand on this spot, "Baby, I want to die here." Everything she relays that her husband says to her is prefaced with "baby." As in, "Baby, you can only eat In and Out Burgers once a week so you don't get fat." This, to the woman who weighs all of 90 pounds soaking wet. Hmmm. I don't remember seeing In and Out in Bangkok, so I guess it's mostly a non-issue. Unless she likes McDonald's or Burger King as much. Nothing can compare to In and Out though.

It's gotten dark already as we make our way back to the bungalows. Madame doesn't turn on the lights because all of the electricity has to go to the noni trees at night to keep the bugs off. Still, she and her workers don rubber boots and hike through the orchard and pick off the bugs by hand. They insist on a pesticide-free noni product. I've seen gallon size bags of these bugs that have been fried up for snacking. I'm told they are delicious and I swear I will try them some day. I'm just not ready.

No lights mean an early bedtime. I'm lucky Madame's husband isn't there because I get to sleep in their bed, which happens to be the most comfortable bed ever, with the freshest, cleanest, smelling linens in an open-aired (Bali-style) bungalow. This will be the brother's living quarters once the main house gets built. I wish I were the brother.

While I'm always leery of bathroom facilities in Thailand, the separate hut designated for bathing is equipped with all the modern amenities but is built out of bamboo with mostly open walls that gives one that feeling of showering outdoors effect. The only soap I could find in the big basket of toiletries was skin-whitening soap, so I guess I'll be going for the albino effect.

The next morning I start my day with a huge cup of coffee sitting out on the open-aired kitchen, more like a deck, really. I'm looking out over the pond as the sun rises over the mountains and I feel the greatest sense of peace I've felt since being in Thailand. I'm thinking of quitting Peace Corps and signing up to be Madame's housewife, or other help. The work wouldn't be so bad. Madame is such a clean freak she cleans up after the maid anyway. And despite having a maid, you can find her sweeping away and cleaning every morning. This is good because she has four dogs and one cat.

The plan for today is to drive to the market and the Cambodian border. During the two-hour drive I witness a kind of poverty I haven't yet seen in Thailand. Upon arriving at the market the sisters won't even let me out of the truck. They tell me it's because it's really, really hot and it smells really, really bad. At least I can now add Cambodia to my list of countries I've visited.

We drive home again and finish the day with a swim in the pond. It's too deep to stand anywhere so it's swim or sink, literally. Somjai doesn't swim so they've rigged up a couple of empty plastic gas cans with a rope and she paddles around as if she has real floaties. The water feels like bath water. But I wouldn't know about that. I've never seen a bath tub in Thailand.

Despite the pleasant feeling of the pond water, I'm a little afraid of the fish. Somjai's husband and brother regularly pull out some decent sized fish that become many of our meals from this pond. I don't want my toes nibbled on. I know people pay to have their rough skin chewed off by little fish, but the idea freaks me out. The sisters insist it doesn't happen here. I insist there's a first for everything.

The next day, eight of us, including the maid and her two children, pile into the truck with a big picnic lunch and head off to a waterfall. I've been dying to go to a waterfall ever since I've heard other volunteers brag about their outings to Thai waterfalls. Was it everything I hoped? Almost. We couldn't stand directly under the falling water because the rocks were too slick to climb there. But there were plenty of pools with falling water to play in and the surrounding trees were lush and junglesque.

Some guys drinking beer out on a big rock pointed to me and said "farang" plus something or other, that I later gather was quite derogatory. My new response to all Thai people who point at me and call out "farang!" is, "*Mai chai farang. Khon Thai.*" (Not farang, Thai person). This is just to be funny and brush it off. But Madame got really angry with them. She was cussing them out and scolding them for being impolite. I don't even want to know what they said that got her so mad. She apologized to me and told me they didn't know any better. She instructs me that the good comeback is to call them Lao. Apparently it's an insult for a Thai person to be called Laotian. I'm thinking maybe it's not a good idea to get into name calling, nor very becoming of a PCV to use what amounts to racial slurs.

When it's time to go home, I'm invited back for the

following weekend to celebrate Madame's birthday. Her husband will be there so I'll get to meet him. I plan to invite Mark, even though his Thai is so good it always makes me look bad. Then I have to explain why I can't speak Thai as well as Mark. I try to imagine two guests from another country in my home, with one guest speaking English much better than the other. Would I ask one, "Why can't you speak English as well as your friend?" Um, no.

I'm going to pack extra bags, just in case they invite me to move in permanently. A girl can dream.

Chapter 22

Bag O'Burgers from McDick

DESPITE ALL THE DRAMA, I still go to the municipal office for a couple of hours every Friday morning, begrudgingly. In fact, the only point I can really see is to make my supervisor feel important. I don't remember that as part of the Peace Corps job description, but I'm thinking it's a good idea to include it. Or maybe it should even be one of the rules, along with always wear your bicycle helmet and never, ever ride a motorcycle. Rule #3 could be, "Always assure important members of the community that they are indeed important." It's a challenge because I joined the Peace Corps to help the underprivileged, not stroke the egos of power trippers. I have come to accept that when dealing with foreign powers, one might need to do the latter in order to accomplish the former. It's a steep learning curve, but I'm discovering the problems inherent in a culture that is firmly rooted in hierarchy and the concept of status. People are either trying to prove their importance or getting upset because someone hasn't shown them enough respect.

My latest dilemma involves my dear giggling Dick. Dick is the student who attends my adult class, brings me green pudding sandwiches, and drives me home every night. She's actually an English teacher at an elementary school with which I'm not associated. She has begged me and begged me to come to her school and help her teach English. It's her first year as a teacher and her English, is, well, kind of like my Thai. She is so darned nice that I agree to finally go one afternoon, knowing all the while it was going to make a bunch of other people angry. Why? Because I somehow belong to them and therefore should not be working with others or helping at other schools. Yes, people actually fight over me like a couple of dogs tugging on a rag doll. But here's the thing. I came here to help people. Rule #25 (or whatever) of PC training is to find where help is needed, and this Dick really wants my help. Furthermore, this time slot was my free time, uncommitted elsewhere, which I'm hoping is still my choice how to spend. So when Dick shows up at my doorstep with bags, not a single bag, but several bags of McDonald's food, asking again if I will come, how can I refuse. God I love this woman.

So I tell Somjai that in my free time I will be going to Dick's school to help. She tells me NOT to tell the supervisor because he will get mad. Later, Somjai calls me. Principal is upset, worried the supervisor might find out and get mad at Principal. Really?! I had to bite my tongue really, really hard

Wai-ing Ronald McDonald

so as not to say something really, really bad about where I think the supervisor can go, or where he can shove it, or what he can go do to himself.

Instead, I take a deep breath. I tell her I will handle the supervisor. If he finds out I've been "messing around" on them, he should contact me directly. Somjai can tell I'm angry, so doesn't pursue it. The things I put up with for McDonald's.

Chapter 23

The Mall

THE BIG CITY KORAT, being only a 30 minute bus ride from my town, has proven to be a great escape for me. Korat has a huge supermarket, where I buy Somjai's beloved peanut butter and other items that can't be bought in our town. It also has a mall. A bona fide, Western style mall with countless shops selling everything from clothes to electronics. It even has a food court.

The food court is where I learn all kinds of fun facts about Thai eating habits. For example, at the ice cream shop in the food court, you can't get ice cream in a cone, but you can get it in a hot dog bun. It gives a whole new meaning to the concept of ice cream sandwich, doesn't it? But what would your ice cream sandwich on a bun be without the Thai favorite topping? Is it whipped cream? No. Chocolate syrup? No. Sprinkles? No. It's corn. As in kernels of corn, fresh off the cob. The corn is usually served under the ice cream, however, in a dish.

When Somjai and I go to the mall together, we always eat at her favorite shop in the food court, which serves Vietnamese food. Somjai grew up near the Vietnamese border which is why she is so fond of Vietnamese food. It's also why she speaks English so well. She was a girl growing up during the Vietnam War. Her father worked in some capacity where American military were often at their house, giving Somjai plenty of opportunities to practice English.

Somjai knows how much I miss farang food, so one day, when we plan to go to the mall, she tells me she's ready to try McDonald's. In the past, she's steered me away from McDonald's, telling me it's too expensive. I think really she was afraid to try it, like how I feel with frogs, fish brains, and the like. But that Somjai, bless her heart, is a trooper! At the age of 43 she will have not just her first taste of McDonald's, but her first ever hamburger. (No cheese, though. She's absolutely disgusted by cheese.) What does Somjai think of her first hamburger that she was so afraid to try? She loves it.

While feeling terribly guilty for being such a bad influence, I console myself with the argument that it's my sworn duty as a PCV to share American culture, the good and the bad. At the same time, I feel like a drug dealer who has just turned on a new customer to their first shot of heroin or something.

The reason we're at the mall this time, is because Somjai insists I need proper shoes for teaching. I've never seen Somjai wearing shoes with less than a three-inch heel. What, pray tell, does she consider proper for me?

Before arriving in Thailand, Peace Corps gave us very clear instructions on appropriate dress. Thai culture dictates that people in certain jobs dress *riap roy*, which is something like our concept of "business," "business-casual," etc. Therefore, women PCVs are required to wear some form of sandal. Given the fact that we ride bicycles every day, and are walking all over in god knows what kind of muck, our sandals can be practical. No Birkenstocks, but Tivas are okay. So most of us wear the most comfortable, practical, sandals we can, what one might call "sensible" shoes.

Somjai insists my sensible shoes are all wrong. Once again, we argue. Once again, it's the battle of the wills. I tell her high heels are bad for your back and feet. She counters with the fact that she's never worn anything but high heels and her back is fine. Her feet never hurt. I insist that if I wear shoes like hers my feet WILL hurt. She insists that's only because I have a "big bootie." She knows because she has a friend who has a big bootie like mine who doesn't like to wear heels either. I switch tactics. I remind her I won't be able to ride my bicycle wearing high heels. She tells me I can just leave them at the school and put them on there.

I crack under the pressure and she wins this round. In the shoe store I can't help but be enamored with the selection of cute, stylish, high-heeled shoes. I wonder if this love affair with shoes is hardwired into a woman's DNA. It's hard to choose from so many, so I end up with not one, but two new pairs of high heeled shoes, on sale of course. I'm embarrassed to admit it, but I love them. Never mind that I'll most likely fall off of them and break an ankle before I ever get a chance to get sore feet or a bad back.

Did I mention the mall has a water park right outside its doors? Since Somjai doesn't swim, she doesn't take me to the water park. I'm dying to try those slides but am too scared to go alone so I come up with a plan. I call up Mark, who can also easily get a bus from his town to Korat. We make a plan to meet there and try the water park. For some reason, it seems that when Mark and I get together, the result is always some form of humiliation, either for me or for him. This time it's both of us who end up humiliated. When everyone stares at us as we go down the slides, we assume it's because we are the only white people there. But this time, the staring includes pointing and laughing. After a few runs down the slide we finally realize we are not just the only white people going down the slides, we are the only people over the age of 12 going down the slides. It turns out Thai adults don't go down water slides, at least not at this water park. To make it worse, men in Thailand wear only Speedos for swimwear. Never shorts. In fact, there's not a pair of shorts to be seen anywhere, except on Mark, who happens to be wearing bright red, long, surfer-style swim shorts. He vows to buy a Speedo assuring me how good he's going to look in it. I vow to never return to the water park.

Chapter 24

The Real Work Begins

As we gear up for the school session to start, Somjai comes to my house regularly to lesson plan. She sits on my bedroom floor for hours, where the air conditioner keeps us cool and comfortable, writing out by hand lesson after lesson, occasionally looking up to ask me for an idea for an activity that is not rote instruction or just translating an English sentence into Thai. That is my "real work," after all, to help Thai teachers with Western teaching methods.

"Amy, how would you teach the sentence, 'Give me a pencil.'?"

My work is cut out for me.

Finally, school starts up again. The real work begins. The first day of school there was an unexpected visit by the "higher-ups" who went around inspecting the whole school. Surprise! Principal got busted because the school looks like a dump (their words, not mine) and because two teachers were absent from classes with no replacements. For the record, there are no janitors in Thai schools. Students and teachers are responsible for keeping the school clean. One can imagine how that turns out. Although you do see the children with their Thai-style brooms that look like the Quidditch brooms from Harry Potter sweeping away every morning as teachers threaten them with a stick. As for the missing teachers, there's also no such thing as a substitute teacher. All I know is that I heard really loud children from one of the rooms and when I looked in I saw students running around and literally rolling around on the floor wrestling. One student was even out on the ledge outside the window of the third story floor! I almost had a heart attack. I wonder if perhaps safety reform should take precedence over education reform. This school would be a lawsuit waiting to happen if it were in the US.

At the end of the day I go to the principal's office to check in on her.

"How are you doing?" I ask in Thai.

She gets out her electronic dictionary and showed me the translation.

"Resign."

I pat her shoulder and nod sympathetically. Yeah, we've all had those days.

I mostly observe classes in my first days in the school. I help a little with pronunciation and lead a few rounds of Simon Says. I work with three English teachers at School 1 three days a week. That's the name of the school. School 1. While observing the first grade class for a while the first day I notice one of the girls has a crying kindergarten student on her lap. It's her little sister on her first day of kindergarten. I don't think she's impressed with kindergarten. They start at age three. I was impressed however that the school let her big first grader sister, all of six years old, hold her and comfort her, while first grade class just carried on.

At School 3 (I don't work at School 2) where I go to help on Wednesdays, I have my most recent bout of "I can't do this! I want to go home!" Despite several invitations, the one English teacher with whom I am paired to work at School 3 never met with me to discuss how we would work together, what we would do, lesson plan, etc. She happens to be the teacher who didn't get her principal's signature because she was fighting with said principal, getting Somjai in trouble with "the office." I have never even visited this school.

So I show up on the first day at School 3 for the first time telling myself, "I can do this. How bad could it be?"

It was a freaking nightmare.

All day this teacher, an English teacher, kept talking to me in Thai. All day I kept saying, "I don't understand."

Finally I called up Somjai at the other school for some translation. She reminded the teacher that I was there to observe and help, not to take over the classroom, which ended up being the easiest solution and by the end of the day is exactly what I did.

How fascinating that students were learning English from someone who doesn't speak it. Let's just say they had been getting a lot of practice writing English words. The optimist in me is thinking that I've really got my work cut out for me. I can really accomplish a lot here. And maybe I will be forced to learn some Thai since not a soul at this school speaks a lick of English. The pessimist in me is thinking yeah, and maybe pigs will fly.

The next day, I was never so glad to see Somjai and the others at School 1. If I've learned nothing else, I've learned to appreciate the very smallest of blessings, like someone speaking a little bit of English.

Once I get into a rhythm of going to the schools every day, except Fridays, my office day, I actually feel like I'm doing good work. At least if I consider baby-steps good work, and continue to remind myself, it takes time. Even though I've been in Thailand five months, my real work has only just begun. I help out a lot with pronunciation and grammar correction or whatever other help is needed. For example, one day Somjai was passing out a worksheet that was teaching the phrase, "You should better…," as in "You should better eat healthy food." Another teacher started a lesson about "turn on and turn off, "only to demonstrate by opening and closing the window while saying, "Turn on the window. Turn off the window." My biggest challenge is always managing the behavior with such large groups of young children. I am tempted to threaten them with the stick. Instead, I raise my hand and physically zip my lips close and wait for 30 little first or second graders do the same. They do! If I'd actually had training in elementary school education I'd have other tricks that I later witnessed, like "1, 2, 3, eyes on me."

The biggest problem is that since I'm so big on clapping hands and chanting everything I teach, those poor kids are going to go out into the world of English, start clapping and chanting to the rhythm, "Would you like some coffee?" "Would you like some coffee?"

One whole day this month is dedicated to giving thanks to teachers. It's like teachers have their very own Thanksgiving Day devoted to them! It's called *Wai Kru* Day. "*Wai*" is bowing in respect like when Thais greet each other. *"Kru"* means teacher. All of us teachers sit up on a two-foot high platform while every single student in the school, in groups of 10, approach the platform, kneel, bow, and give us bundles of flowers, incense and candles. The whole ceremony felt super special. But watching the little three-year-old kindergarteners learn how to perform the ritual for the first time was absolutely adorable. I almost split a gut laughing. Then the poor cuties had to just sit there for two more hours of the ceremony. I could not believe how well behaved they were. The three-year-olds in my family could never sit still like that without some entertainment.

From the adult English class beat, the newest student to join my class was actually a foreign exchange student in Indiana when he was in high school. He went to a private

Catholic school where Sister Theresa would always give him detention because he didn't understand the rules and so was always breaking them. This must have been after the days of nuns hitting with rulers, which he would have been more accustomed to. He may be the only one here who has a clue what it can be like for me here.

Chapter 25

Heads on Fire and Other News from the Bangkok Post

EVERY DAY AFTER WORKING AT THE SCHOOL I ride my bike to the shop that holds the Bangkok Post for me. The first thing I do after I go home and take my splash bath to cool off is read my newspaper. It's one of my great pleasures. It never ceases to amaze me what news makes the Bangkok Post. Tacoma's chief of police killing his wife. (My sister lives in Tacoma, WA.) An earthquake in Western Washington. (I went to college and taught high school in Western Washington). Not to mention, I can see the scores from every single Seattle Mariner's game. (I am a fan). If I didn't know better, I'd think the editors at the Bangkok Post know a farang from Washington State is living here and they are therefore catering the news to me. I even saw a Dear Abby letter from a woman in Yelm, Washington, which is a 30 minute drive from where I went to college in Olympia. I'm suspicious of these letters supposedly written from my neck of the woods. Why do they use the term "Mum" instead of "Mom"? Perhaps it's the editor who obviously learned British English and not American English.

Of course I also get interesting news from around the world, like from China, where a man was performing voluntary castrations on his kitchen table.

The photos in the Bangkok Post can be shocking; they'd never make the local newspapers in the US, or even The New York Times. Take for example the photo of the British soldiers in Iraq showering in the middle of the desert. At least it was taken from behind. I even cut that one out to save, you know, because it was so "interesting."

I also learn a lot about current events in Thailand. For example, while the drug war in Thailand that lasted two months and claimed 2000 lives was deemed a victory by the Prime Minister, the headlines these days feature the war on "dark influences." They mean the mafia.

One Thai man has been arrested for trying to sell materials to make a dirty bomb. Turns out he's a school principal. I have a hard time imagining my principal associated with any kind of bomb, except maybe the "f" bomb after watching one too many American movies. No time for dirty bombs when you're off meditating in caves. But I guess you never know, especially given all the stress she's under.

Then there's the horrifying. I opened the paper one day to find two separate pictures of people with their heads on fire. Literally. The photo showed them with their heads aflame. I just stared at the photos for the longest time. It didn't seem real. But it was. The caption under the woman read, "She later died." No shit? Her head was on freaking fire!

This is just a small example of how violence is regularly portrayed in the Thai media. Back when I lived with my host family and actually had access to a TV, I was mortified nightly by the news and the images of bloody, mangled, dead bodies in all manner of gore and disfigurement. Every night as we watched the evening news we saw victims of gun shots or car accidents or other tragedies lying dead in the street with blood everywhere. What's worse, is seeing the family members nearby screaming or crying in agony. It was appalling. I had always been disturbed by America's problem with glorifying violence in movies, in video games, in sports and music. I was convinced most Americans had become desensitized to graphic images of violence. I thought I was desensitized. I know I am desensitized…to fictional images. These real life (dead) images are too much. Once I saw a woman sitting next to the dead body of her husband in his coffin. This is just not an image we'd see on the nightly news or in an American newspaper.

In fact, we Americans in general are blessedly protected from real images of violence. The violence we hear about on the news is often tragic, or heart-breaking, even mortifying. However, American media outlets censor these images. This is a kind censorship. The positive takeaway is that at least I now know that I, for one, am not desensitized to bona fide images of violence.

Violent images on the screen in Thailand would continue to haunt and perplex me throughout my stay. It seemed such a paradox, such a peace-loving society, where almost everyone are followers of Buddha's peaceful teachings, so strict they won't euthanize animals even in the most dire of circumstances. Yet violent images are everywhere.

Jungian psychologists would say this is an unconscious expression of "the shadow", the dark, ugly, hidden part of ourselves. The part of ourselves that we refuse to acknowledge. This only partly helps me understand.

The worst experience I had regarding Thais' response to violence was in a movie theater where I was watching a Thai movie with English subtitles. The movie came highly recommended. However, all I can remember about this movie was that it included a horrifically graphic gang-rape scene. This was not the first time I'd seen a gang-rape scene in a movie theater. Watching "Last Exit to Brooklyn" years before made me physically ill. It turns out I'm not as desensitized as I thought. But what disturbed me more than watching the rape scene in the Thai theater was all the laughter from the audience. Men, and women, were laughing hysterically. At a gang-rape. Any nausea I felt from the scene was soon overcome by my rage at the audience. I was so disgusted at the Thai people laughing at the screen I turned around and glared as hard as I could, trying to shame them with my stink eye into sobriety. Failing at this (no one even made eye contact with me), livid and shaking, I got up and left. It was the first and only time I have walked out of a movie theater.

I held onto that anger for a long time. Years later I still feel angry at the memory, even though I understand now that laughing is actually Thai people's way of handling discomfort. Even with that knowledge, I found this behavior an unforgivable outrage. Sometimes cultural understanding can never be enough to overcome our judgement. Cultural sensitivity draws a fine line between what can be deemed as okay, because it just happens to be their culture. Consider forbidding women to drive, or stoning, or even capital punishment in the U.S. Of course what's most important is to remind oneself that despicable behaviors can be found in many cultures. It doesn't make them a "bad people." It makes them flawed humans. Something I happen to have a lot of first-hand experience with.

Chapter 26

Why Thais Need Glasses

IT'S 6:00 P.M. ON A SUNDAY NIGHT and I'm lying on the hospital bed of the emergency room of my town's hospital. I was dropped off in the parking lot by some guy on his motorcycle, who pointed me in the general direction. His is not the driver of the motorcycle that hit me as I was riding my bicycle home. That motorcycle is probably still along the side of the road along with vegetables strewn everywhere. It was actually a motor scooter that hit me, not a motorcycle. I briefly consider that I could be in big trouble for violating the number one safety rule for PCVs. Never, ever ride a motorcycle. I guess I should have waited for a truck to pick me up off the side of the road. Oh well. Too late now.

A nurse approaches me on the bed and starts to wipe some dirt off the scrape on my hand that I hold up to show her. It's not my worst injury, but for some reason it's the one I show her. I ask her if she knows Dr. Sombat.

"He knows me." I tell her in Thai, remembering that Dr. Sombat speaks fluent English.

"What's his surname?" she asks.

How the hell do I know? She leaves without finishing cleaning my hand, let alone examining the huge raw patch of flesh on my shin. I'm scared because I don't have my phone with me. I don't have any ID with me. Feeling a little in shock, I'm not sure how many more Thai words I can bring from my brain to my mouth.

Then a stranger is by the bed. A woman. She takes hold of my hand, talking to me gently in Thai. I nod as if I understand, but I don't. There are blood stains on her coat. Yes, she is wearing a coat. Apparently Thai people feel cold when they are riding their scooters or motorcycles. I'm wondering, is it her blood? She doesn't appear to be injured so I don't think so. Is it my blood? No. My wounds aren't bleeding, just scraped, raw patches where the skin was left on the pavement. Then I see the little boy. He's standing quietly beside her. He's staring at me intently, not sure what to make of me. Then I remember, it's his blood on the woman's coat.

I flash back to the accident. I was riding my bicycle on the dirt path along the side of the road. Next thing I know I'm on the ground.

"*Katote ka! Katote ka!*" (I'm sorry! I'm sorry!) A woman is helping me up.

As I sit up and look around, my bicycle is lying on its side, wheels still spinning, with its poor little basket smashed flat. Vegetables are strewn everywhere. I see that a little boy is sitting on the ground as well, looking stunned. His nose is bleeding. After attending to me, this woman, his mother, wipes his bloody nose with her jacket sleeves.

Then people are stopping on the road, in their cars, their motorcycles. The people in the houses across the street run out and I'm glad for a second to see a familiar face. It's a man from my "stage performance" days, the MC if you will. He helps me up and says something about the hospital. He helps me onto the back of a motorcycle. I don't really care at the moment that Peace Corps could send me home for this safety violation. It was only a one-minute ride to get to the hospital anyway.

Now I'm scared because I've been sitting in the hospital bed for a half an hour and still no one is attending me accept the stranger holding my hand and the little boy whose nose has stopped bleeding. Finally the MC from my stage days shows up and I ask, "Do you know Somjai?"

He indicates something affirmative so I'm trusting that he's summoning Somjai. He apologizes for not being able to speak English, then miraculously remembers a word and tells me, "Wait!" Like I'm going anywhere. Which reminds me of something and I ask the stranger holding my hand, "*Jakayan tii ni?*" (Where is my bicycle?)

She answers something I don't understand as she brushes away the flying insects trying to congregate in the raw flesh of my leg. I appreciate the gesture, and conclude from the ensuing behavior that she did not intentionally mean to hit me on my bicycle. She tries to explain, but the only words I can understand are "didn't see, didn't see." Apparently not. I try to muster a smile. She's obviously feeling pretty bad about the whole thing. I mean, who wants to be known as the woman who took out the farang volunteer on her bicycle? She probably was worried the whole U.S. was going to be up in arms that a Thai would "attack" one of their citizens. A citizen on a mission of peace, no less.

More time is passing and it's still just the two of us, plus the little boy. Occasionally I tear up when hit with a wave of pain or fear. She just keeps talking away and brushing bugs away, so I try to talk to her.

"*Jep mai?*" I ask her if she's hurt.

She assures me she's not.

"*Moto-cy okay mai?*" Yes, that is proper Thai grammar for "Is your motorcycle okay?"

She doesn't know and she doesn't seem concerned about it. Then there's more awkward silence.

I ask her how old her little boy is.

He's six.

Is he hurt?

He's hurt a little bit.

No one at the hospital has attended to him yet either, which concerns me. This poor little guy just crashed into a farang on bicycle and while his mother was wearing a helmet, which is not typical, the little boy was not wearing one, which is typical.

I ask him his name and give his arm a little rub, smiling at him. Maybe he's scared and will feel better. But as he begins to answer, the doctor finally enters and asks in English, "Can I help you, please?" I'm guessing his English is also a little rusty.

Then chaos erupts. I start to see a bunch of familiar faces running through the hall, teachers from the school, their kids, the janitor, a cook from the cafeteria. Word on the teacher row has gotten out. Seven or so people are peeking their heads in over and under each other. I don't want them to see me crying like this. They'll laugh at me, and I'm not in the mood. I know they are concerned about me, but they'll show that concern by laughing, because they feel uncomfortable. It's one of the cultural characteristics I find hardest to stomach. Especially because they often laugh at small children who are crying, which breaks my heart, and makes me angry.

But no one is laughing now. Despite the comfort at seeing all these familiar faces, not one of them speaks a lick of English, so I'm still shit-out-of-luck.

Finally Somjai comes running in, which makes me cry more. She embraces me and gives me a Thai kiss on the cheek, which is a quick, gentle rub of the nose against the skin with a sweet little inhale, like they are smelling you. Only it's a kiss. My first!

"Aim-eeee!" She's exclaiming in that tone that always sounds like I've done something wrong. "Are you okay?" She starts to tear up, too.

"Yes. Yes." I assure her. "Please go get my phone. It's at my house, in my room." I want to call Peace Corps headquarters right away.

Meanwhile, the Thai doctor is finally examining me. He is annoyingly jolly as he tells me to bend my knee. I do.

"Can you bend your elbow?"

I can and I do.

"Good! Nothing is broken! You only have superficial injuries! You are fine!"

Um….

"Um…My shoulder hurts." I explain, attempting to elicit a more thorough examination.

He goes behind me and starts palpating my shoulders.

"Does this hurt?"

"No."

"Does this hurt?"

No.

"This?"

No.

"Good! Nothing is broken! You are fine!"

Um. Okaaaay.

Some of the teachers come in closer as the nurse proceeds to clean out my abrasions.

"*Mai pen rai*," they say. "*Mai pen rai.*" Sometimes this means never mind, as in, no big deal. I hope they mean "don't worry, you are okay." But when it comes to cleaning the gravel from my raw leg, I'm not feeling like I'm okay. I'm brave in many ways, but when it comes to pain I'm a total wimp. Never one for stoicism in the face of discomfort, I yell out loud in protest.

The stranger who hit me, who no longer feels like a stranger, grasps my hand even harder to draw my attention away from my painful leg. It all feels like too much. I'm wishing I had skipped the hospital altogether and just walked home.

Finally the leg wound is cleaned and dressed and I'm released with an antibiotic and Tylenol. A policeman is waiting in the lobby to take statements from me and the no-longer-a-stranger who hit me.

Somjai translates in somewhat less fluent English, "What do you think of this?"

She trusts that I'm a mind reader, as I often have to be, since it's easier for me to read minds than understand Thai language. Somehow I do know that I'm expected to explain what happened.

Everyone looks at me expectantly and breathes a huge sigh of relief as I respond and Somjai translates, "It was an accident."

No-Longer-A-Stranger explains her version of what happened to the cop and Somjai translates for me. She has told the policeman that because it was starting to get dark, and because my skin is so light, she could not see me.

Even as my eyes widen and my jaw starts to drop in disbelief, I can tell from the look on everyone's faces that I'm expected to accept this version as the policeman and everyone else has. So I nod in agreement.

"What do you want to do about this, Aim-eeee?" Somjai asks. "What this woman did, it is like, it is against the law."

I shake away the brief inclination to take advantage of a teaching moment to explain to Somjai the English term "press charges." Instead I shake my head vehemently no, grasp No-Longer-A-Stranger's hand and squeeze it tightly, repeating, "It was an accident."

Another collective huge sigh of relief. Somjai looks at me gratefully and says, "You have a good mind." I know she means she thinks I've done something good by not pressing charges. Did they really think I would? Apparently from the anxious looks, wringing of hands, and sighs of relief they did.

Somjai told me No-Longer-A-Stranger would be checking in on me. That she was taking care of getting my bicycle fixed and paying my hospital bills. I didn't feel bad about this because medical care in Thailand is extremely affordable. It's called "The 30 Baht System." It means people pay 30 baht per doctor's visit, including emergency room visits. That's less than one dollar U.S. I was pretty sure bicycle repair was affordable as well.

After what seemed like lifetimes since I'd limped into the hospital, Somjai finally drives me home. She wants to spend the night with me. I wasn't even polite.

"No. No. No. Absolutely not." I was fine and I wanted to be alone, like a cat, to nurse my wounds in private.

"Let me look in your refrigerator to make sure you have food…I only see soy milk. That's not okay."

"Somjai, I have tuna fish, peanut butter, and bread. It's fine."

"Please can I stay the night? You might need help."

"Thank you. No. I promise I will call if I need anything." I'm practically pushing her out the door.

"Okay, Aim-eeee. I will keep my phone on." She reluctantly backed out the door and drove away.

I was finally able to call the Peace Corps doctor who offers to send me transportation that night to get me into Bangkok to be checked out. I assure him I'm fine to spend the night here and that I can get myself to Bangkok in the morning.

Despite all my proclamations that I am fine, my body is quite beat up. The Tylenol does nothing for my pain so I sleep little that night. I can't sleep on my shoulder, and with every restless toss or turn, pain from some part of my body jolts me awake. Daylight finally comes and I hobble out to the street to flag down the earliest bus.

A thorough exam from Peace Corp Thailand's official doctor determines my shoulder is indeed sprained, the ligaments pulled and stretched. Most of my bruises and abrasions, while painful, are not serious, with one exception. The hand-sized patch on my shin where the skin is missing is actually like a burn, explaining why it's so painful. It hurts to walk because the skin is trying to regrow and gets stretched with any movement. It gets cleaned and wrapped three more times the several days I stay in Bangkok. I hate having it cleaned and wish we can just leave it wrapped and alone until it heals. Every time it gets cleaned it feels like it's being set on fire again. Did I mention I'm not good with pain? Thankfully the Peace Corps doc gives me Percocet and I'm finally able to sleep.

Over 10 years later I hear a report on the news that Thailand is the second most dangerous country in the world for driving, with the second highest number of fatalities. Why am I not surprised?

While recovering in Bangkok, I have some time to think about my Peace Corps goals. Ironically, it's the accident that helps me "see" the problem. Eye sight. Was it my light skin that kept No-Longer-A-Stranger from being able to see me as it started to get dark? Or was it, perhaps and more likely, her poor eye-sight?

We take vision correction for granted in the U.S. Our eyes are tested every year in school. Even babies in the U.S. are diagnosed with vision problems and are prescribed glasses. In Thailand however, almost no one wears glasses. Not a single student at my school wears glasses. Surely it's statistically impossible that zero out of hundreds of young people have vision problems. Certainly even more adults would need glasses. But they're not wearing them. How many accidents happen because of drivers' poor eye-sight? Is eye-sight even tested as part of the driver's license test?

I begin to wonder, is it the cost that keeps them from wearing glasses? Is there something I can do as a volunteer to help them get glasses? I know for a fact Americans have a plethora of old glasses they no longer use because their eyes have gotten worse. Countless pairs of used glasses that end up where? Why not match these glasses to Thai people who desperately need them? I have no idea how to implement this plan, but the seed has been planted.

I wished that as a condition of me not pressing charges that I'd required this woman have her eyes checked. It sounds like a joke, but it's very serious. She hit me directly from behind on a straight stretch of road. There was no corner, nothing blocking her view. Light skin or brown skin, she should have been able to see me right in front of her. Then again, maybe the little boy's head was blocking her view. Either way, Thais need glasses!

Despite all my whining, moaning, crying and complaining, one thing is clear. I am so very lucky. I am so very grateful. With no doubt this accident could have been much, much worse. The doctor tells me the sprained shoulder could have easily included broken ribs. He says many of the other bruises could have been broken bones. He tells me that the ever-so-painful abrasion from a slide against the pavement is much better than an impact injury. Furthermore, I could have hurt my head. Even worse, the little boy could have been injured or, with no helmet, worse.

I wonder if the little boy, years from now, will remember the accident. "Hey Mom. Remember the time we took out the farang on the bicycle?" And they'll laugh about it. Thais often laugh about the things that make them uncomfortable.

Chapter 27

The Outsiders' Perspective

I END UP STAYING IN BANGKOK for about a week to recover before returning to my site. It's not that my injuries are that bad. But I'm unable to ride my bicycle while my leg is growing new skin. I can barely walk. It's helpful to be in Bangkok where I can access food easily. I'd be of no use at my site anyway. Not to mention, I would have to rely on Somjai and the others for everything, which is distasteful to my sense of independence.

Peace Corps has generously put me up at the Taewez Guest House. It's a modest, but comfortable youth hostel that has become Peace Corps volunteers' favorite place to stay when they are in Bangkok due its proximity to the Peace Corps office and budget friendly pricing. Rooms go for about $8.00 per night, but you can upgrade for air conditioning and bathrooms with real toilets if you pay a little extra. The staff at Taewez is incredibly kind and hospitable, and meals are prepared and served at very reasonable prices. I'm content here at first, and then I'm ecstatic because of the books I've scavenged from the Peace Corps volunteers' trading library. Thailand has hosted thousands of volunteers over the years who bring books with them from the States and/or have them sent by friends and family. After reading the books, volunteers generously donate them to the library in the Peace Corps office. After selecting several appealing titles, I seclude myself in my room and enter my happy place.

I'm lying in my bed, escaping into a fascinating story about a man who spent a year on the Mekong River, when I hear a timid knock on my door. That's weird.

"Excuse me, but Peace Corps people are here." A Thai-accented voice speaks softly through the door.

Peace Corps people? Do other volunteers happen to be in Bangkok during the middle of the week? That would be highly unusual. Is somebody else injured?

So I go out to greet my fellow volunteers, but instead I am faced by two total strangers. In the briefest sizing up I can tell these are not Peace Corps volunteers. I don't even think they're American. What is going on here?

In the next second, Imran and Natasha are introducing themselves with accents that confirm my initial assessment. "We are with Peace Corps Macedonia. We work in the office."

Macedonia? Wow. I had actually hoped I'd be assigned to Macedonia when I was applying to Peace Corps and asking for an Eastern European placement. Macedonia was my very first choice. Why? Because it borders Greece of course! I've always dreamed of going to Greece.

Imran and Natasha explain that they are in Bangkok for a training next week. I remember hearing something about this. Peace Corps was planning to revamp its whole financial system and people from the finance offices of various different countries would be in Bangkok to learn the new system. Imran and Natasha came early for a little vacation. They had always wanted to visit Thailand and have just now arrived.

I immediately sense their frustration as they talk over each other in perfect, if accented, English, about how hard it was to get to the guest house. How a taxi was stopped at a traffic light for a whole 30 minutes. (They are not exaggerating. I know the light!) How they tried to get to the Peace Corps office but the taxi couldn't find it (again, no surprises). How they finally got out and walked to get to this guest house which was recommended by the Peace Corps office. How they haven't been able to communicate with anyone. (They are wondering why no one speaks English.) How it's really hot here (they noticed?) and how Natasha especially does not have a good first impression of Thailand. And no, she will NOT take her shoes off before entering the guest house, custom be damned. "I just can't do it," she insists.

Ohhh…kaaay. I'm worried as I get them checked in that they will be unhappy with the accommodations. Taewez Guest House is clean and comfortable and many of the rooms have AC and bathrooms. But it's no three star hotel. I'm relieved when they express satisfaction, admitting decent accommodations are hard to find in Macedonia. Who knew?

I'm sucked in, fascinated.

"Tell me more!" I beg, explaining how I had originally requested Eastern Europe as my first choice for placement with the Peace Corps.

When they ask me why Eastern Europe was my first choice, I explained that I when I was a high school teacher, assigned to teach Western Civilization, I felt woefully ignorant about this part of the world, especially given all the changes due to the collapse of the Soviet Union.

"You knew Macedonia was part of Yugoslavia, didn't you?"

"Um, no."

"You knew about the war there, though, right?"

"Some. It was in the news a lot when I was younger." I'm embarrassed to admit I paid little attention to current events in the world at that time in my life. I was preoccupied with "finding myself" and other hedonistic pursuits.

As they share their perspectives on their part of the world, I start to wonder if they are even talking about the same place.

Their viewpoints diverge immensely. I try to tread gently with my questions. Whenever Natasha answers, Imran jumps in, "No, Natasha!" and vice versa. This kind of passionate discourse is most refreshing for me. After spending so many months in a country whose people, to quote my Thai trainers, "don't like to talk about important matters. They don't like to argue. They would rather talk about toothpicks."[6] In general, Thai's will avoid challenging another's remark in effort to "save face." It's a kind gesture. They don't want to make the other person look bad.

Meanwhile, these Macedonian women are practically yelling at each other in front of me, a veritable stranger. I love it. I continue to ask questions.

"What religions are practiced in Macedonia? Wasn't religion previously outlawed?" I had picked up some "facts" from the high school textbook I had used.

"No!" exclaims Natasha.

"Yes it was, Natasha!" argues Imran.

"I come from a mixed background," explains Natasha. "My father is Jewish and my mother's family is Christian."

"By Christian you mean…?" I start to ask.

"Orthodox," she interrupts.

"Oh yeah! Greek Orthodox!"

"No! No! We are not Greek. We are not Russian. Just Orthodox. Greece doesn't even recognize our country so I will not even travel there."

What a shame I think. I hear they have awesome beaches.

---

6 Of course, like all statements regarding culture, this is a massive generalization. Somjai and many of my Thai language teachers seemed to enjoy talking about "important matters." Once when my sister came to visit, she got into a bit of an argument about George W. Bush who was the U.S. president at the time. My sister was critical of G.W. My student, a middle-aged Thai gentlemen, was arguing G.W.'s merits. However, even as the discussion got quite heated, the Thai man kept a smile on his face. That's when I started to learn about the concept of Thai smiles having many different meanings.

"My family always celebrated the Christian and the Jewish holidays," she continues. "There was no problem."

"You are wrong, Natasha!" Imran is ethnic Albanian. A Muslim. "There was definitely a problem when my family wanted to fast for religious purposes. Furthermore, I wanted to go to college and study Albanian but I couldn't."

This went on and on and I got lost in the argument until they finally agreed to disagree, acknowledging that they simply come from different perspectives. Years later as I reflect on this argument I wonder, if these two women from such drastically different backgrounds can live together, work together peacefully, agreeing to disagree, then Americans who have different viewpoints should be able to do the same. I wonder how they could get to this point. I wish I had thought to ask them that at the time.

Then I ask, "How about Peace Corps in Macedonia?"

"We have 18 Peace Corps volunteers in Macedonia."

I practically choke on my water. Eighteen? Thailand will have over 100 when the next group arrives next week. No wonder it was hard for me to get placed there. Of course, Macedonia is quite a small country.

"What do the volunteers do there?" I ask.

"Mostly teach English."

I don't say anything, but I'm wondering why they need English teachers if Macedonians speak English as well as these two.

A couple of days later, as it's time for us to part ways, Imran and Natasha share some fascinating insights.

"I think volunteers in Macedonia have it a lot easier than in Thailand," Natasha confides.

"Natasha! Stop with that!" Imran scolds, clearly uncomfortable with how Natasha's insights might make me feel.

"No, please continue," I say. "I want to hear more."

"It's so difficult to communicate with people here. (It is!) And the language seems very hard to learn. (Indeed!) It's so hot. (Amen!) It gets hot in Macedonia, but not like this. And it smells bad. (Preach, sister!) It's so difficult to get around! Why can't the taxi drivers find the place when you give them the address? (I'd never thought to ask. To me, it just is what it is.)

Hearing all this is like a drink of cool water to my thirsty, parched throat. Despite Imran's concerns for my feelings, hearing Natasha share about the hardships I face every day in Thailand is validating, even comforting. Someone understands how hard it is! It's not just me! I'm not just a big baby, whiner, wimp! Okay, maybe I am a bit of wimp. And a whiner. But still. This outsider's perspective was a gift. I'm glad I had the accident and had to stay in Bangkok.

Chapter 28

Fruits of my Labor

WHEN I RETURNED BACK TO MY SITE and my home, Somjai showed up first thing with my newly repaired bicycle. I had no idea of the extent of the damages. I only noticed the morbidly smashed basket, which was bad enough. I really loved that basket. But the returned bike had not only a new and bigger basket, it was even decorated with a lovely Playboy bunny decal! It had new pedals, new brakes, and a new rim. Absent, however, were my rear view mirrors. Oh well, who can complain about luxuries like rear view mirrors on your bicycle when you've got a brand new Playboy bunny decal? The accident was almost worth all the pain just to have that decal on my bike.

When I show Somjai my still somewhat raw looking abrasion, she insists I stay home the next day, and all the rest of the week for that matter. This is ridiculous, I'm thinking. But I don't argue. I can always just show up at the school on my own accord. She sends her husband off to buy me dinner and takes the broom from my hand, as I had started to sweep up the lizard poop that accumulated in my absence. She insists on finishing the job for me. I teach her the phrases "If you insist" and "I insist."

The next day Somjai shows up with my lunch, as promised. Another teacher is with her who gives me bags of fruit. She's very impressed with how much better my leg looks, but says I must not come back to school yet. Imagine trying to keep skinned-knee children home until the scab is all gone!

She tells the other visiting teacher how I had cried at the hospital. My guess is, she's trying to accentuate how bad the accident was. I decide not to get mad that she's tattling about my being a cry-baby. Later Somjai returns with dinner, my newspapers, and a phone card. The ladies who work at the store where I get my newspaper every day insisted on coming to visit as well. They brought Diet Coke, which they only stock per my request. I don't even like it, because it's not real Diet Coke, but Coke Light, which tastes nasty to me. But bless their hearts for their kindness anyway. They also brought cake and bottles of water.

"She cried," Somjai points out again. Again I trust she's indicating the severity of the accident.

The next day, two teachers from my other school show up with lunch for me, as well as bags of fruit. I haven't even put a dent in the first bags I received, but I appreciate the gesture immensely. At this point I have watermelon, pineapple, oranges, guava, and rambutan.

That night Somjai brings dinner again and I realize I'm getting awfully comfortable with this kind of service which continues the next day. That afternoon I'm visited by more teachers who bring, what else, fruit! Now I have apples, too. The stickers say they are from Washington. One of the teachers had come to the hospital right after the accident.

"You cried," she reminded me.

Heck yeah, I cried. It hurt like a mother, okay? You would have cried too, I think to myself. Or maybe not. She probably would have laughed.

I learn that No-Longer-A-Stranger has come by my house several times while I was in Bangkok. Finally, she found me home and had all kinds of treats for me. Cans of tuna fish, crackers, and grapes, because no get well gift is complete without fruit. She tells me it was a good thing she hit me instead of someone else. She is a divorced single mother with three kids to feed. If someone had pressed charges she would have struggled to pay. She had never even met a farang before, let alone crashed into one with her motor scooter. She says she's glad I was so nice. I think perhaps my work here as a volunteer just might be done!

I also receive a visit from the man in my adult English class who had been the exchange student in the U.S. He brings me fruit *juice* (phew, no more bags of fruit) and a necklace with a Thai angel pendant for protection. I think he's telling me he had some sort of premonition about my accident but I'm not sure. I'm supposed to wear the necklace at all times to protect me from bicycle accidents and other bad luck. We have a lengthy discussion about the spirit world, which had me so scared I couldn't sleep that night for wondering about ghosts. I wasn't sure if the angel pendant I was wearing included protection from ghosts.

One might think that I've milked this injury business to the limit and I have. I just sort of got sucked into it. In the years after I return to the states I will end up having a total of five surgeries, if you include the C-section with the birth of my child. With each surgery I was homebound, bedridden and in pain. While one friend of the family brought a meal one night after I had my baby, that was all I received as get well gifts. Did I receive any Diet Coke or fruit? Not a measly little grape. Of course I know many Americans are good about bringing food to people in times of need, especially with a death in the family. My family and circle of friends, apparently not so much. Which is not to criticize them, (I am no better), but to point out the cultural difference. I can't say enough good things about Thai hospitality, generosity and kindness. They are such a caring people. Which is why I forgive them for all the references to my crying in the hospital.

The abrasion starts to look much better and Somjai agrees to "let" me come to school. Mostly I need to escape the bearers of fruit visiting me at home every day. My first hour at school Somjai calls me into her room. Six of the office staff I teach on Friday mornings were there to see me. They had come bearing gifts. Three bags of….you guessed it…FRUIT!

Chapter 29

More Trouble with Tokays

Despite my bicycle accident, I've been blessed with very few health problems. No dengue fever yet. I've only had a total of one cold since I've been here and that was because I went to visit a bunch of volunteers and didn't sleep all weekend. Turns out Red Bull has caffeine. Who knew? I don't even bother to heat the water for washing dishes anymore, which is still done in the bathroom for lack of a kitchen sink. I don't see the point when nowhere else where I eat uses dishes that have been washed with hot water. I must have some immunity.

I am not immune, however, to the skin problems that we were warned in training are the biggest health issues for volunteers in Thailand. I've had my share of rashes and fungus. But heck, I have those problems in the U.S. as well. What caught me off guard was the dreaded "Peace Corps Acne." I had it, and I didn't even realize it until I showed up at school one day with two whole pimples on my face and one of my co-teachers generously informs me that I have acne and should go to the hospital. For two zits?! No, no, no, no, no. I've had enough of hospitals for a while and will not be returning because I have a couple of zits on my chin. Somjai was kinder. She asked if a mosquito had bitten me and accepted my blemish explanation without further harassment.

I have also had a problem with little shards of broken glass in my feet. I may be one of the only people who can say they've broken a glass on their shower floor. This is of course a result of my washing the dishes in the bathroom which has come to seem totally normal. A smarter person would wear flips flops into the bathroom. I just kept thinking that surely all the glass would be gone, and then, "Ouch!"

Despite all these minor issues, I'm thankful for good physical health now that I've recovered from the bicycle accident. My mental health is another story. When I returned to my home from Bangkok, just when I thought I'd overcome everything that could possibly make me snap, I am faced with my greatest challenge yet. Lizard poop.

Now, the little gecko turds are one thing. They are like dried up bird poop that you can sweep and mop right up. Sometimes it requires some scrubbing, but it's not smelly or anything. It's a fact of life everyone deals with in Thailand. However, one day I noticed a smell coming from my kitchen. I checked for spoiled fruit. God knows I had to throw away enough after the deluge of get-well gift bags. But I couldn't find any spoiled food. Then I saw it. A slimy, nasty, unmistakably big ol' piece of poop on my kitchen wall. I really almost lost it.

It took me awhile to figure it out, but when I heard the distinctive cuckoo clock chime that evening, I put two and two together. My friendly tokay had returned, and to show his displeasure at having been so rudely evicted, he was using my kitchen wall as his personal toilet.

I heard about this woman living in Bangkok who went bona fide insane because she couldn't control the ants in her house. I get it. Only for me, it will be tokay poop.

On a positive note, remember that the tokay is supposed to be good luck. Therefore, I'm glad he's back, even if he refuses to be housebroken. I'm sure I wouldn't have gotten hit on my bicycle had I never thrown him out in the first place.

More good news! One of the geckos had babies! Quite cute, actually. I feel like a proud grandmother. I have to enforce the house rules for the little ones. When one tries to sneak into my bedroom I nudge him out gently reminding him only humans allowed in the AC room. I briefly consider naming them, then I realize it's pointless as I can't tell them apart anyway.

Chapter 30

Teacher Training Superstar

MR. (BAD DOG) SANIT took a job in Bangkok. Because the teachers who were given his English classes speak zero English, I volunteered to teach those classes on my days at that school. These are grades one through four. I've gone from teaching academic essays and discussing symbolism in literature with teenagers in the US to singing nursery rhymes and teaching the alphabet. The little *"dek deks"* are so stinking cute I just want to pinch their little cheeks every day. Then they start to misbehave and I'm far less enamored by them.

It would seem I'm becoming somewhat of a permanent fixture around the school. Random students regularly approach me in the "halls" to talk to me. One group of little girls have become so unselfconscious as to closely examine my skin, my shaved legs (Thai women don't shave as they don't have enough hair on their legs to warrant it), and the hair on my arms (Thai women don't have any).

Like most volunteers, teaching English doesn't make me feel like I'm accomplishing as much as we'd set out to do. The challenge is to find other ways to help, assess the needs in the community and work from there. I've asked everyone I know in the US to send me old glasses they're no longer using. But then what?

As a way to learn more about how volunteers can contribute to their communities, I join Peace Corps Thailand's Gender and Development (GAD) committee. Traveling to Bangkok for the monthly meetings is an unexpected perk of this committee. I connect with volunteers from the group that arrived the year before my group. They invite me to a teacher training they're conducting in one of their towns. Of course I say yes. I always want to take advantage to learn from other volunteers and I'm dying to see more examples of volunteer-led teacher trainings as they can take so many different forms.

When I arrive in this town, I'm dismayed to learn the only transportation from the bus station to my hotel is a *som lor*. A *som lor* is the Thai version of a rickshaw. A skinny Thai man with sinewy calves who weighs a fraction of what I do, pulls the heavy farang and her bags on a bicycle. When we go up a hill I'm so worried he's going to have a heart attack trying to pull me that I almost get out and offer to pull him instead. If I decide to quit Peace Corps, I may become a *som lor* driver. By the look of his physique it would be a great weight loss plan.

That night in the hotel, I join my "senior" PCVs in a hotel room for the planning of the next day's training, writing the schedule and who's leading what activities on a huge piece of poster paper they tape on the wall. I'm impressed with the focus and maturity of these volunteers. I'm at least 10 years older than all of them, and the only one of the bunch who is a trained teacher, but they take on the task with confidence and skill. Peace Corps has obviously done a great job of training them. Of course, just because they're not trained teachers, doesn't mean they don't have excellent organization and facilitation skills. Which I soon discover, they do. They have one flaw, however. And that's I where come in. It doesn't have a thing to do with my training or experience as a teacher.

They ask each other who will lead the songs. No one volunteers. It turns out they all hate leading songs. This is a problem because Thai teachers expect songs. Songs are paramount in teaching English, not to mention songs are fun. Well, for some of us songs are fun.

"I can lead songs," I volunteer.

"Really? You don't mind! That's awesome! Thank you!" They are clearly surprised that I am so willing to do this. Thank goodness we all have different strengths to share!

When it was all over I was again so impressed with the other volunteers' professionalism and dedication. It was truly inspiring. Even more so, they want me to come to all of their trainings from now on so I can lead the songs! It feels really good to be appreciated and valued.

I'm inspired to facilitate a similar teacher training in my town. A big one, for all three schools.

*   *   *

I'm told that if the principal from School 2 dies, god forbid, my principal from School 1 will now actually attend his funeral. Previously, she had sworn that if he died, she wouldn't attend. This is all because of me. This is the kind of contribution I make to the country of Thailand as a Peace Corps volunteer. We all do what we can. The news of this has put me in a great mood. Or maybe it was the McDonald's that one of my former students brought me as a get well gift. Of course I'm perfectly fine at this point, but I'm still receiving visitors bestowing yet more fruit and McDonald's.

But how did I accomplish this feat of getting my principal to attend the funeral of the other principal, should he, God forbid, meet his demise? It was my planning the teacher training for all three schools in my town. I'm sure I'm losing something in the translation, but still. The power is starting to go to my head.

Chapter 31

"We Feel so Fun and Get Many Things"

Sung to the tune of "When the Saints Go Marching In":

Oh English Camp!
When we come in!
Oh English Camp when we come in,
We feel so fun and get many things.
Oh English Camp when we come in.

ONE THING I'VE LEARNED is that English Camps are "a thing" in the Peace Corps world. I have attended my first of many, along with ten other volunteers and two-hundred and some students. We had songs and dance. We had games. We had crafts. We felt fun![7] A perk for me was that the volunteers were dismissed in the evening to go hang out together while the Thai teachers supervised the overnight camping. After at least one hundred rounds of "Oh English Camp!" we felt we deserved the break.

Thai people just love a camp. Of course I had heard of band camp, art camp, and sports camp. I'd even attended basketball camp back in my youth. But I personally had never heard of a foreign language camp. Since then, I've done my research and found that you can find a kids' camp for almost

---

7 Now with years and years of teaching English as a Second Language under my belt, I'm not fazed one bit when I hear "I feel fun" because it's such a common error among second language speakers. At the time however, I found it absolutely hilarious.

any foreign language you want your child to learn. To me, real camp was Girl Scouts' camps.

In fact, Scouting, for both boys and girls, is so popular in Thailand that every single student is a member of the Girl and Boy Scouts of Thailand. Once a week, instead of the school uniform, the students and teachers don their Scouts' uniforms. I have to tell myself not to try to make Hitler Youth connections when I see the students and adults in lines, marching in matching uniforms. I was a Girl Scout after all, until I made peace with the fact that I hated crafts and wasn't real big on camping either.

Peace Corps volunteers long ago figured out that the camp was a great way to sneak in community action. I read one Peace Corps memoir whose author had served in South America. There, it was "clubs." In Thailand, we have camps. Since my eyeglasses project was not taking off like I had hoped, I needed a different mission, a cause about which I not only felt passionate, but could also achieve success. Camp was where it's at. But not the run of the mill "we feel so fun and get many things" English camp. My mission would be Life Skills Camps.

Back when I was recovering in Bangkok from my bicycle injuries, I had ample time and opportunity to explore the resources in the Peace Corps office. I kept stumbling upon manuals for conducting Life Skills Camps. I wasn't really sure at first what that was, but I liked the sound of it. Who couldn't use life skills? The more I researched and learned specifically what was taught at Life Skills Camps, the more I was determined to facilitate one.

Life Skills, of course, run a huge gamut of things to learn. With youth in Thailand, areas of focus have typically been goal-setting, decision-making, alcohol and drug awareness, and the ever popular sex-ed, including STD awareness. I had found my calling.

I took my idea back to Somjai. I would easily be able to organize and manage the curriculum for the camp. Logistics and funding would require Somjai's help.

Like all good friends, Somjai and I had had our share of conflicts. Most recently I was angry with her for an episode at the English camp. This was the first time Somjai had interacted with any other of the PCVs. In the car with another volunteer, Somjai heard this farang say "turn left" in Thai language. Two whole words in Thai. Imagine my horror when she loudly exclaims, "Oooh! Aim-eeee! Your friend speaks Thai better than you! Aim-eee, you must learn, too!" To the amusement of my fellow volunteer, Somjai went on and on about how poorly I speak Thai. Of course, this was true, but that wasn't the point. The point was, here in a culture that caused me no end to grief because of the need to always save face, she was obliterating my face in front of my fellow volunteer! Furthermore, I happen to know how to say those two words also, if not as eloquently as my American colleague.

At lunch the next day Somjai heard another PCV say something in Thai and she started in again about how terrible my Thai is and how I need to get a tutor so I can improve. I discreetly told her we would discuss it later, reminding her it was impolite for her to say this in front of my friends. Yes, now I was obliterating her face, but I was angry.

"Oh! Oh! Sorry! Sorry!" she apologized. But I'm quite certain the apology was not for hurting my feelings, but for making a social faux pas in front of the Americans.

I owe everything about my experience in Thailand to Somjai, but truth be told, she was a difficult colleague. I told myself regularly that was the price I paid for working with a fluent English speaker. All of us volunteers had our challenges. I also appreciated the opportunity to work on my "people skills" by not only getting along with Somjai, but making the most of our relationship. However, we struggled with my goals as a volunteer on a regular basis due to her nature and her reputation in the community.

Somjai once told me that the other teachers hate her. I consoled her by explaining they were just jealous because she is such a good teacher. Which is, in part, true. The other part of the story is they say she thinks she's better than everyone and that she sucks up to the principal. So she's like the "teacher's pet" only she's the "principal's pet." We all know how we feel about the teacher's pet. Especially if they tend to be bossy and a know-it-all to boot.

Thai shower in school.

The bottom line was, for good or bad, I needed her to accomplish my goals, I depended on her. And despite my frustration with her, I appreciated her immensely.

Somjai was often resistant to my ideas. I was asking a lot of her, forcing her way out of her comfort zone. But I could always cajole her into doing what I needed.

I hate asking for money. Seriously, even if it's for the best of causes. It has a lot to do with how I was raised and old childhood issues I never got over. So I could understand when Somjai was resistant to asking for money as well. But first and foremost to pull off a Life Skills Camp we needed funding. Of course I could have asked everyone I knew back in the States to donate a small amount and we could have easily funded the camp that way. I wouldn't have even felt bad about asking for that. However, that would be a failure on one of the most important tenets of Peace Corps projects. Sustainability. A Peace Corps project can be the most amazing, most helpful, most life-changing project, but if it's a one-time deal that can't be replicated once the volunteer is gone, it's not considered successful. It wasn't sustainable.

So while a Life Skills Camp felt easy as pie for me to make happen, I was flummoxed on how I was going to make it sustainable. I knew I needed to start with finding local funding. Would the school district actually fund the camp? Somjai didn't want to ask.

Somjai was always getting in trouble with the school district supervisor. Not because she did anything wrong, but for quite the opposite reason. She was too good at her job. There was tremendous jealously regarding her ability to speak English so well and her relationship with me. I was supposed to have a stronger relationship than I did with the supervisor as my community connection. But as noted before, my inability to speak Thai and his inability to speak English made that impossible. I take responsibility. I failed at learning Thai. Somjai had a lot to do with that failure, but she also suffered greatly for it. Take this example: It came time for her to submit her quarterly report. (Oh, how the Thais love those long-ass handwritten reports!) When she candidly reported that "Amy is not able to do community outreach service because she doesn't speak Thai" it was interpreted as "Somjai is the only one who can work with Amy because she is the only one who speaks English and is therefore better than everyone else."

Getting funding for the Life Skills Camp wasn't going to be easy, but I was determined.

Chapter 32

Bit Term Bai Tiow

(Midterm Vacation Trip)

To MY GREAT SHAME, instead of hanging out with the teachers in the evening as they eat snacks and gossip, I retreat to my room to rejuvenate. So to assuage my guilt, when I'm offered an opportunity for some real engagement with my community, and possibly some fun, I jump on it. It's the *bit term bai tiow!* That is, the midterm vacation trip. I'm thinking it's something like spring break, Thai style. As I understand it, this is an annual trip sponsored by the city mayor for all 70 teachers to be transported by tour buses on a vacation. So many things to love about this country!

This trip happens to be to "the beach." The beach? I'm so in! Thailand is famous for its beautiful beaches on which tourists from all over the world come to vacation. I'm also promised there will be lots of karaoke and dancing. It could be really fun, or my worst nightmare. I'm maintaining a positive attitude, reminding myself I will be IRB (Intentional Relationship Building) while seeing more of the country. I might even learn something.

I'm assigned to bus #8. Eight buses? For 70 people?

A slight misunderstanding again. The bit term trip is not only for teachers, but everyone in the community is invited. That means nine buses will be holding 500 of my town members and taking them to the beach. What the…?

We board the buses at midnight. This is a timesaving travel trick. You get to sleep (supposedly) on the bus, saving a day of travel and saving one night's accommodations fee. I wasn't looking forward to the night on the bus. Unlike Thai people, who always sleep on buses, day or night, regardless of the noise level, I am never able to sleep on a bus. But I really knew I was doomed when as we headed off into the night the driver turned on a video of a comedy show. All Thai buses are equipped with TVs and DVD players. The comedy show would have been perfectly fine except for what is my least favorite thing about Thai culture, and their insistence on always, ALWAYS turning up the volume to the highest, most painful decimal possible.

I read recently that one way to get prisoners of war to talk, or in other words, torture them, is by playing certain music really loud, like Metallica or the Barney song. If a Thai person were receiving this torture, they would love it. They'd join in singing aloud happily. They'd probably say, "Turn it up! Turn it up!"

But for me, riding a Thai bus is my own private torture, as I alone seem to have any issue with the noise. Never mind that it was well after midnight and many of the passengers were sleeping. After about an hour of this torture someone had the good sense to request some quiet time for sleeping as we weren't due to arrive at our destination until 7:00am.

I offered a silent prayer of thanks to that person and tried to get a little shut-eye, which might have been possible if Thai buses were at least a tad bit warmer than the inside of a refrigerator. Don't get me wrong. I love air conditioning. I consider it one of the greatest inventions ever, right up there with Pepsi in a bag. Air conditioning is one of the reasons I've been able to endure living in weather that reaches over 100 degrees daily. But that doesn't mean I can sleep in 30 degree air conditioning. I was even wearing a sweatshirt, as I have learned the hard way, a sweatshirt or jacket is a must-have on a Thai bus. My teeth chattered as I shivered through the night. Finally, at 5:30am, which is considered a quite reasonable and appropriate time to start the day, everyone else started to rouse.

Finally, rest stop! Even with the nine buses splitting up and stopping at different rest stops one can imagine the lines waiting to use the squat toilets. This was just the first of several early morning pit stops where the drunk guys who had been partying all night on their bus, fueled with their liquid courage, approach me wanting to practice all two of the words they know in English. In the U.S. such a scene might be cause for some sort of embarrassment or discomfort. Here, it was par for the course and simply laughed at.

Another misunderstanding I had about this annual bit term vacation was that it is not just a trip to the beach. Oh no. Instead, it's an adventurous tour with stops at historic palaces, temples, and the requisite souvenir shops. Not to sound ungrateful, but I was in this for the beach, the whole beach and nothing but the beach, which was taking far too long to reach with all these tourist stops. I was getting impatient when finally, after our lunch stop, which you can imagine took a little time with 500 people, we did arrive at the beach.

While this was not one of the famously gorgeous tourist beaches of the South of Thailand, it had sand and it had ocean and I was thrilled to be off the bus. Once we check into our room I start to head for the beach when Somjai tells me, "First we will take a nap."

I almost laughed out loud. The hell we will! It was already afternoon and we were slated to leave first thing in the morning.

"I didn't come all this way to take a nap in the hotel."

"Okay. Okay. We'll go to the beach," she agrees begrudgingly. But she wouldn't leave the shade of her umbrella, citing concern for her skin becoming dark. I think not being able to swim was also a factor for her not getting into the water. Furthermore, knowing her love of seafood and eating in general, I think she was perfectly happy to eat crab and other kinds of food the vendors were bringing around. They sell beach-goers everything from beer to seafood to trinkets. You know you're on a Thai beach for native Thais when:

- no one is actually on the beach but hiding out under big umbrellas which can be rented for about 50 cents.
- a total of maybe 15 people out of 500 actually get in the water.
- the only people wearing real swimsuits are under six-years-old and everyone else's swimwear is baggy t-shirts and long, Bermuda shorts, even the lone farang.
- the water must be at least 90 degrees.
- total strangers invite you, the lone farang, to join them riding the six-person banana boat pulled by a jet ski.
- other total strangers call you, the lone farang, over to take a picture with them.

My fun in the sun was followed by a dinner party for all 500 people with the promised karaoke and dancing. They twisted my arm until I sang, and the men in the front started handing me 100 baht notes. Had I not seen this practice before, I'd worry I was expected to start a strip-tease, but I assure you, I kept every stitch of clothing on, and had collected a total of 700 baht for singing one song. That's about $18. But I wasn't finished with my earnings yet. During the dancing there was a spin-the-bottle contest. Not THAT kind of spin the bottle. This is more like musical chairs. When the music stops, the dancers make a circle. The mayor's wife spins the bottle and the person the bottle points to when it stops spinning wins 100 baht. I won twice!

The farang earning all that money was the talk of the town the following day. Weeks later, I still had strangers approaching me in the market asking how much money I got singing and dancing. I had totally forgotten the rule about volunteers being forbidden to accept money. Oops.

Chapter 34

A Miracle?

"**Pleeease, Aim-eeee! Let's not do this!**" Somjai pleads.

We were getting ready to walk into the Rotary Club meeting in Korat. I had learned that the Rotary Club in Thailand, like in the US, was a possible resource for sponsoring our life skills camp, or at least donating something to support it. I had spent considerable time persuading the very resistant Somjai that we needed to approach the Rotary Club in Korat. I was shamefully unsympathetic to Somjai's resistance. I didn't understand why she was so afraid to ask them for money, nor did I try to understand. I was goal-driven. I would have made a good CEO.

"Pleeease, Aim-eeee! Let's not do this!" Somjai pleads. I was literally pulling her in her high heels and short skirt to the entrance of the meeting. I thought she might cry.

As most things in life, the fear in anticipation of this event was so much worse than the actual event. Once we got into the meeting and sat around the table, Somjai was able to compose herself and give her spiel about why the Rotary Club should give us money. Of course, the meeting was all in Thai and I understood none of it. I didn't even know they had refused us until after we left and Somjai told me they had said no.

Although we hadn't achieved the result we wanted, Somjai was elated. She point blank told me that she was proud of herself for doing something she thought she couldn't do. She had overcome a fear and learned she had abilities beyond her imagination.

Again I considered that my work here might be done.

But no, it had just started.

As I dress in my finery and high heels and slap on some lipstick I ask myself, shouldn't I be in jeans and a t-shirt digging a ditch or planting a garden somewhere instead? We are off to see yet another community VIP to beg for money for the camp. This time it's the mayor. We wouldn't dare disrespect him by showing up dressed in anything less than our finest. He offers us wine coolers as per custom. We decline. Maybe that was a mistake, because after we make our case, he turns us down, too.

I even ride my bicycle to the hospital and see if Dr. Sombat has any ideas. I'm secretly hoping he would be kind enough to offer his own support, but he doesn't. Nor does he have any ideas for whom I might ask.

When we finally exhausted all of our ideas for whom to solicit for funding, Somjai had decided the camp was not meant to be.

"*Mai pen rai, Aim-eeee*," she cajoled with obvious relief that she might be done with this business. "Just let it go."

Because I was as discouraged as Somjai, I almost did. Then fate intervened.

Ever since I'd arrived in Thailand I was sending regular mass-emails home to friends and family regaling them with my trials and tribulations in Thailand. The process of writing was my therapy. The support my friends and family sent in their replies was my lifeline.

When I wrote of my dilemma in finding local funding, a miracle appeared in the form of an email reply. One of my dearest friends back in San Diego, Lisa Gaffney, said she had a work connection in Thailand. If that wasn't miracle enough, the connection wasn't in Bangkok or any ol' random place in Thailand. It was a company located in Korat! This was huge. The company was an American tech company called Seagate, and the fact that they were local meant they would be much more likely to help us.

When I thought my luck couldn't have gotten any better, I learned my friend's connection at the company wasn't the stereotypical male Thai boss, but a bona fide woman. Of course, females in position of power were becoming more and more common in Thailand, but I saw this as an especially good omen. Women in the technology industry were not common in Thailand. This woman must be exceptional to say the least.

I emailed this woman introducing myself, explaining my role as a Peace Corps volunteer and Gender and Development Chairperson. I gave a brief description of the life skills camp with its objectives for helping youth make and achieve goals.

Her email back stated that our life skills camp was something she and Seagate were interested in supporting. She asked if I could come meet her at the office with Somjai for more details and a thorough explanation in Thai along with the detailed budget proposal.

After I explained all this to Somjai we just kind of looked at each other in disbelief. After all the stress, all the begging, all the blood, sweat and tears (okay, there was no blood), we had gotten so used to being turned down we were actually in shock. Could this really be happening? Plus, we dare not get our hopes up until we had actually received a commitment.

Unlike all of the other times we went out begging for money, Somjai was giddy with excitement this time we went to Korat. It helped that this time we brought the principal with us as well as two students, two middle school girls, to help plead our case. Now that I was the point of contact, it took all the pressure off Somjai.

Similarly to all the other times we asked for money, this meeting was all in Thai. Somjai had chosen her two top female students and had them memorize a spiel about why they needed life skills. I'm not even sure what they said, but they were poised, solemn, and earnest. And they must have said the right things because she said "yes!" In fact, she was so impressed and supportive of the idea, she said that even if Seagate wouldn't sponsor the camp, she would personally support it herself.

We were still in shock and couldn't believe this was really was happening. And yet we were elated. I hugged and thanked the students. Somjai and I hugged and squeezed each other's hands. We had done it!

"Congratulations!" I told everyone. "Now let's get this life skills camp started!"

Thank you again Lisa Gaffney, for everything. Your love, friendship and support has meant more to me than you will ever know. I dedicate this chapter to you, my friend. Cheers!

Chapter 35

Sweatin' in a Winter Wonderland

AH YES, "WINTER," OR "THE COLD SEASON" as they call it in Thailand, has arrived in full swing. What does that mean to the average person in Thailand? If you are a Thai by blood it means you don your winter coat and complain about how cold it is even though the temps are hovering around the low 70's. Brrrrrr!

If you are American or some other brand of farang, you are probably more comfortable than you've been in a long time.

If you're somewhere between farang and *kohn Thai* (Thai person), like I consider myself after a year here, you vacillate between truly enjoying the cool breeze and then relating to the Thais who feel too cold. I even wore my coat while teaching last night. My biggest complaint is the early morning cold water splash bath. It's a little too refreshing these days.

If you're a Thai child, your nose is constantly running.

If you're a snake, you're dead on the side of the road. I have counted up to ten dead snakes on a one mile stretch of highway. Not nearly as many as the frogs that were run over on the road during the rainy season, but still. And since this is a new phenomenon as of late, I assume it has something to do with the cold season.

If you're a rice field, you are no longer the beautiful green stalks shimmering in the wind but are now brown, harvested stubbles which will soon give way to the dry dirt fields.

If you're the dirt from said fields, you're leaving layers and layers of dust all over my house because it's so dry and windy.

If you're a tokay living in my house, nothing has changed except you seem to be urinating more frequently indoors, leaving big yellow puddles on my kitchen floor.

If you're a female Tesco-Lotus employee, (Tesco being a European version of Walmart with stores all over Thailand) you are forced to dress up as Santa's helpers and are forced to listen to Christmas music all day long even though you are Buddhist.

So obviously the cold season in Thailand corresponds with the American holiday season. Holidays can be especially hard for volunteers who may be spending their first Thanksgiving and Christmas away from family. To assuage the homesickness, the Program Director hosts a traditional Thanksgiving dinner at his home in Bangkok for all the volunteers. We feel much like a family so this is truly special and something for which we are all thankful. What's more, turkey dinner baby!!!

Many of us from Western culture would associate the phrase "the birth of our king" with Christmas, or maybe even Elvis's birthday. But in Thailand you'd be mistaken on both counts. We just celebrated the king's birthday, a federal holiday, which resembles our own Christmas in many ways. Along with larger than life pictures of the king put up all over town were thousands of Christmas lights, framing the pictures and covering all the trees. Similar to traditional Christmas celebrations, the actual ceremony involved getting dressed up, singing, praying, candles and gifts. Only instead of under the Christmas tree, the gifts for the king were placed under his picture. And we weren't gathered in a church or even a temple, but in a parking lot.

The highlight of my evening was a mass of bugs drawn to the street lights in the parking lot descending on us like a plague of locusts, covering our clothes in bugs of all sizes, mostly of the grasshopper or cricket variety. If I were prone to such thinking, I might wonder if the God of the Old Testament was punishing us for worshipping "false gods." I began to amuse myself by counting how many bugs actually landed on different people. I counted 27 on one woman's back, but it's possible I missed some. Somjai pointed to some grasshoppers on one woman's back and exclaimed excitedly, "Oh, those are my favorite to eat!" Less amusing was when they landed down my shirt, or worse, up my skirt. Surely for some this is the stuff of nightmares. Lucky for me, I'm rather fond of the bugs.

From the teaching beat, I gave an oral assessment to my students this week. They wrote their English names that I had assigned them on the top of their papers. When I came across one that had the name "Santa" at the top, I was confused.

"Somjai, what's this? I didn't give anyone the name Santa."

She calls the kid up to me, wearing his name tag, which says Santa. He's grinning from ear to ear.

After she asks him about it, she translates for me. "He didn't like the name you gave him. He wants to be Santa."

"What do you mean he didn't like the name I gave him? Tommy is a very good, respectable, American name! If he tells people his name is Santa they'll laugh at him and make fun of him!" I really did have the kid's best interest at heart. But I let it go for then.

Then I came across the name "Lave."

"Somjai! What is this "Lave"? At least Santa is an actual name, sort of. But Lave?"

She whispers in my ear with a patient smile that told me she understood exactly what this boy was going for.

"Amy, he wants his name to be Love. See? He wrote Love on his name tag. He just spelled it wrong on his paper."

Oh. Well. That IS kind of sweet. I let it go.

Then I come across the name "Brush." Yes, Brush. Somjai pointed to the kid who wrote his name as Brush.

"Johnny! Come here!" I demanded. I pulled a brush out of my bag and asked, "What's this?"

"A brush," Johnny says.

"So you know this is a brush. And you want your name to be brush?"

He grinned and nodded enthusiastically.

I sighed. Somewhere in all of my frustration and eye-rolling I learned some very important lessons.

One is about Thai culture. Names in Thailand have meanings that everyone knows. It was important to these kids to have English names that had meanings as well. The meaning could be special, like love, or every day, like brush, as long as there was a meaning.

The second lesson is about my goal here to encourage students to be creative and think for themselves. Who cares if someone would laugh at the name Santa? He chose a name for himself that he thought would be a good name, not one dictated by his teacher. He stood up to his teacher. He challenged his teacher. That is success! Same with Love and Brush. These are good names. These were good lessons.

Chapter 36

Chickens, Lizards and a Rat, Oh My!

Email to my sister Shannon: Hey stranger! Of course now that you haven't asked about my love life, I finally have something to share! Do you believe in love at first sight? I don't think I did until this past weekend. I went out clubbing with Mark in Bangkok and I noticed this very attractive man. Well, to be more accurate, both of our eyes got huge and our mouths dropped open when we saw each other. We were the only non-Thais there. We danced and he kept telling me how beautiful I was, which was music to my ears, even over the blaring club music. He is from Morocco, 28 years old, (I know, a little young for me but oh well!) His name is Mustapha. His English is terrible but he is so, so cute! Oh, and he's Muslim. Not very devout obviously, since we met at a dance club. But considering the US "War on Terror" that recently started I consider it my personal mission of peace to befriend this particular Muslim. I gave him my number. I hope he calls! Love, your smitten sister.

BECAUSE I TRAVEL SO FREQUENTLY, I keep my wheeled backpack in various stages of packed-ness at all times, sitting upright on my dressing room floor. One afternoon I stepped into the dressing room and, imagine my horror, when I happened to notice a smallish tokay crawling around on the outside of my backpack.

"Oh no you don't!" I scolded. "This is NOT acceptable!"

He didn't even flinch, let alone run away. He was breaking every rule of our agreement. My guess is that he was an adolescent tokay. You know how teenagers are. Pushing the boundaries. Testing the limits.

What to do, what to do. I wasn't going near it, so I did what I always do. I ran outside and yelled to the nearest neighbor, who happened to be my 10-year old friend Aa. Poor Aa. She really wanted to help me, but she was no more eager to go near that tokay than I was. With some coaxing, I finally got her to join me. Having her hold the dust pan and small broom, we crept into the room. Lo and behold, the tokay was nowhere to be seen. With a sick feeling, I timidly peeked inside of the backpack. Sure enough, there he was, making his little ol' self right at home among my t-shirts and unmentionables. Ewwww!!! This tokay had taken it too far! I picked up the whole damn backpack and threw it out my front door. By that time, another neighbor had come to help me shoo it out of the backpack. I couldn't shake the heebie jeebies for days.

Finally recovered, one night I got up to go potty in the middle of the night. I couldn't see very well, groggy and without my contacts in. No sooner had I sat down on my elevated squatty toilet to pee when I saw (and felt!) a blur of a furry creature the size of my fist scurry at lightning speed across the top of my feet and scramble down the drain. I'm sure I woke the neighborhood with my scream of terror. To add insult to injury, while the lizards are at least content to feast on the large population of bugs and spiders roaming about the house, this creature has kept its presence known by ingesting whole mangoes left out on my kitchen table and has gnawed through a plastic bag to get to the sliced bread. And don't even think that I will ever repeat the mistake of not tightly screwing on the lid to the jar of peanut butter. I don't think I can live like this. The house is just too small. There's no hiding. I may have to move. The only solution I've been offered is a glue Thai people use to trap rats. I don't know if I can do that. The one positive side to this story is how much I miss the days when it was just the lizards.

Desperate, I called up my landlady. She brought her husband and another man over to cover up the slats in my bathroom with screens. Then they set a trap. They set out a cage with some pork hanging in it to lure any lingering lizards. I loved this idea. Only for days I kept seeing tokays on my walls, but never a tokay in the trap. Maybe they don't like pork.

When I returned home Sunday evening after a weekend away, I opened my door and tried to walk into my house, only I couldn't go in because there was this…poop…everywhere. Now I know tokay poop. And unless my tokays had serious dysentery or food poisoning, this was no tokay's doing. So I tip-toed through the kitchen, avoiding the little messes and find that the whole kitchen table looks like a tornado hit it. Everything's been knocked over, and there is poop all over the kitchen table.

Then I hear a noise, a fluttering, and I see a chicken! In my kitchen! Oh. My. God. What the…???

I ran outside and called my landlady. Again. I tell her there's a chicken in my house. She says, oh yes, a little chicken, right? Yes, I guess it was a fairly small chicken. Wait. How did she know that? She said she'd be right over. She explained that while she was in my house mopping, as she does from time to time, it had started to rain. So she let five, (FIVE!) of these young chickens into my house to shelter them from the rain. When she was ready to leave, she could only find four. So she had only let four out of the five out of my house, leaving one to reign terror on my kitchen and every other room.

Now, for the record, my landlady has to be one of the sweetest, kindest, most caring people in the world. I adore her. Clearly she had been acting out of compassion for the chickens she didn't want stuck out in the rain. But I could not contain my frustration and anger. When I come home from a weekend away, all I want to do is chill, recuperate, and prepare to go to work the next morning. I was obviously upset by this turn of events. She couldn't understand what my problem was. She was just helping out the chickens.

"Chickens don't do anything!" she pleaded. Except poop all over my house, dismantle my kitchen, eat my mangos…

Her husband had to chase down the chicken while I paced up and down the road in front of my house with my cell phone trying to get a hold of friends who would sympathize with this situation. Then her husband comes out of my house holding the tokay trap. It had caught something alright. It wasn't a tokay. It was furry. At least I now knew for sure what the furry blur racing over my feet was. Oh yes, it was a rat.

I see the husband sitting on the motorcycle holding the chicken in one arm, smoking a cigarette with the other hand, the cage with the rat in the motorcycle basket, and it all of a sudden seemed very, very funny. Aa joined me and we inspected the rat in the cage. Do you know that rat actually looked cute and innocent with its big ol' eyes and twitching nose? It wasn't creepy at all. It was just like a hamster or something nicely furry. I had a sad feeling I knew what was for dinner at my landlady's house that night.

I haven't seen any tokays in weeks. No evidence of any rats. Definitely no chickens. It's lonely. I still turn on the hall light and give some time for the tokays to hide before I come into the bathroom. I still look around with trepidation for a few seconds in the bathroom before I go in. But they're gone.

I found some eggs in the slot where the door closes. One was starting to hatch. It was definitely a baby tokay. About an inch long. For about one second I thought about letting it in. Then I thought better, and threw it over the fence. And proceeded to break all the unhatched eggs.

And this just may be my last (sniff sniff) tokay tale.

Chapter 37

Into the Groove: One Year Later...

A YEAR AGO WHEN WE STARTED TRAINING we were given a handout of a graph that represented the emotional rollercoaster typical for a Peace Corps volunteer. I had lost that graph in the mass of a gazillion other handouts they gave us in training. But someone reminded me about it, and it turns out I was right on track. Apparently, after about a year of being really annoyed, frustrated and generally unhappy, the typical volunteer tends to get into the groove of things. You start to feel good about things. You start to deal with the culture shock better. You start to get shit done. Now I understand why Peace Corps asks for a two-year commitment. It takes the whole first year just to get into the swing of things.

The "swing of things," rather than a set routine, is the continual events and activities that keep a volunteer busy. Here's a breakdown of my Peace Corps life these days:

Planting a school garden: By golly, I was determined to make digging in the dirt part of my Peace Corps experience. Alas, I stood around in my high heels and lipstick while the 9th grade students did the digging and planting. I had provided the seeds, though! Literally.

Presentation to new volunteers: Now that I'm a veteran volunteer, I get to take part in the training sessions. I've been asked to present on life skills camps. Never mind I haven't actually facilitated one yet.

Curriculum planning: Somjai and I are preparing for the life skills camp as well as the curriculum for the next term.

It means hours and hours of planning. We were aligning teaching with standards and objectives and assessments, yada, yada, yada, when the superintendent told us we need to put on an English camp. Never mind that we already have a life skills camp to put on. Now, I think I could probably conduct an English camp in my sleep, blindfolded and with my hands tied behind my back. Still, we are required to submit a minute by minute agenda with detailed activities and we have to submit it now. It's not digging ditches, but it does feel like work.

Scout Camp: Every student in my school is a Boy or Girl Scout, from first grade to ninth grade. Every teacher is a Scout leader. Every Thursday students and teachers wear their Scout uniforms to school and instead of bowing when they greet you, they give the three finger Scouting salute. After school they learn to tie knots and stuff.

Every year they hold a traditional Scout camp where fourth through ninth graders girls and boys and all the teachers go somewhere and set up tents and build clothes racks and food racks out of bamboo. This particular year they didn't have enough money to go somewhere cool so they set up the tents and racks in the school field.

For the record, I was a girl Scout and my mom was a Scout leader. We were still segregated back then, so I'm a little shocked to see the girls and boys camping together. I'm even more shocked when it comes time for the nightly campfire. Techno music starts to blare and all the male teachers come out carrying torches, wearing nothing but grass skirts, tribal paint all over their bodies. They are dancing around a fifteen-foot high pile of wood. This would have traumatized me as a girl Scout. But the real trauma would have come when the "lady boy" (transgender) teacher dances up seductively to the superintendent to hand over the torches to light the bonfire. Luckily, Thai youth are much harder to traumatize. Except when it comes to speaking English with me. That scares the shit out of them. I'm sure many of my former students are still suffering PTSD from being forced to speak English with me.

I would have to argue that my Scout camping experiences probably would have been more fun if, like this particular Scout camp, all the male adults plus one female (the PE teacher) had gotten shitty drunk before the camp even started. Of course I was invited to join in the libations. I politely refused. I didn't want to lead on the PE teacher.

In Thailand, gender and sexual orientation, appears to be much more fluid than in the US. Take the "lady boy" phenomenon. While I didn't know about it before living in Thailand, men and boys who want to or feel the need to dress like women are perfectly acceptable in Thailand. In fact, Thailand is quite famous for this. At least all the guy volunteers seemed to have a heads up on it. In fact, the guys in our group were almost paranoid about being duped. Fair enough. Thai *gatois*, or lady boys, are usually gorgeous and convincing. They are accepted members of the community.

In fact, while preparing for yet another festival at the school one day, Somjai was applying make-up to one of our 4th grade boys. I asked her what was going on.

"He's a lady boy."

Well okay then. This was of course way before transgender issues were properly addressed in the US.

So the superintendent isn't fazed at all when the lady boy dances up to him with the torches. It's all part of the ritual.

Environmental English Camp: Just when I had gotten over my bitter resentment towards the eight volunteers who got placed down south in beach towns, I took a ten-hour bus ride down south to help one of those lucky souls with his Environmental English Camp. Yes, it's a thing. And yes, I'm still bitter. Very bitter. That could have just as easily been me living down there on the beach.

But the camp was awesome. We had a beach clean-up and taught the kids all kinds of cool stuff about how to help the environment. We had them chanting, "Reduce! Reuse! Recycle!" over and over and over until I heard it in my dreams that night. Years later, I can't hear "reduce, reuse, recycle" without being taken right back in time to that Environmental English Camp.

Home tutoring: On weekends when I'm not traveling to and from some camp, about eight little ones show up at my doorstep for English lessons. Initially I avoided this practice despite the countless suggestions from my neighbors. I wanted to keep my space private and personal. I was afraid of not having enough time to myself. But after a year here, having time to myself is not a problem, and if I truly am here to help Thai people, why am I gonna turn 'em down when they ask for an hour or two of my time for something they really want, which is for their kids to learn some English? It's relatively painless. The kids range from about five years old to eleven or twelve. I just wing it when they show up. If I run out of ideas, they never get tired of "Head, Shoulders, Knees and Toes."

Lest one starts to assume things are smooth-sailing, let me assure you plenty of drama still ensues. Take the Computer Camp drama. Did I mention camps are "a thing" for Peace Corps volunteers? Somjai and I were invited to bring some students and join some other volunteers for a computer camp. We weren't really sure what that would entail, but it was planned by a good friend of mine, so we were happy to join. Of course in order to take students out of town for this camp we'd need to get permission from the superintendent. After an hour meeting with the three of us, in which I understood, at most, three words of the whole meeting, Somjai explained everything to me.

Somjai had asked the superintendent if we could take a school van to the computer camp. He said no. The reason we couldn't take the van to the computer camp was because so-and-so's wife who is a teacher at the school is jealous of Somjai and thinks she should get to go to the camp instead of Somjai. And another higher up so-and-so does not support five students going to the computer camp because everyone is jealous of Somjai. Everyone is jealous of Somjai because she can speak English and they can't and therefore they can't talk to me, which is apparently a super bummer because I am such an important person. Then so-and-so secretary told Somjai that higher-up so-and-so was saying bad things about Somjai before she came to the office.

Finally, Somjai begs me, "Aim-eeee, please tell them we don't want to take the van."

I never wanted to take the van. I didn't know we were asking for the van. I didn't even know the damn van was an option, but sure, I will tell them we don't want to take the van and we will just take the bus. That was before the I realized the bus would take seven hours compared to the four hours by van, and not realizing one of the students would be throwing up the whole way.

"The bus is fine, Somjai."

"But it is too difficult for me, Amy."

"Somjai, I don't even speak the language and I take the bus somewhere almost every weekend. Why is it too difficult for you?" And so on and so on.

Someone should write a soap opera based on the drama here. It would give "Desperate Housewives" a run for its money. Better yet, it could be a reality show. Instead of "The Real Housewives of Wherever" we could have "The Real Teachers of Non Sung."

Computer Club: If all this wasn't enough, I was also working on getting a computer club started for students who want to learn this new invention called "the internet." Not that I know how to use it myself, but I know how to send an email, which is more than anyone here can do.

And there's still evening English class for adults!

At this point, I was the one who needed some life skills. Time management and stress reduction, anyone? I found Thai whiskey to be pretty effective.

Lunch at school.

6th grade girls.

Chapter 38

Sometimes it's Still Hard

I TRY TO STAY UPBEAT HERE. But sometimes I really hate it here and all I want to do is leave.

I get myself out of bed at 5 a.m. this morning to get to the market before all the mushrooms were gone. I get on my bike to ride the three miles and start sweating immediately, even though the weather feels cool. There is little traffic, but every time I turn on one of the back roads I'm facing packs of dogs, lounging in the middle of the road, looking shifty, seemingly waiting for me. I do a quick u-turn and stay on the main road. I have a healthy paranoia about dog attacks.

I bravely approach the market with its throngs of early comers. I force myself to smile at the staring faces, to politely ignore the pointed fingers and shouts of "Farang!" You'd think that after a year here either the staring, pointing, and "Faranging" would stop, or I'd get over it. Sometimes I'm over it. Today I am not. Nor am I over the *uon* comments. *Uon* means fat and it's used freely to describe any person that is literally bigger than a size two. I, believe it or not, fit in that above-size-two category. I know it's not meant cruelly, but today I hate it. Today I wish I were a size two simply so I would not have to be told I'm fat.

Going to the market is also like going into one of those clothes shops where you are hounded by sales clerks trying to make a sale. Every single vendor is calling out to me in Thai, trying to get me to buy their vegetables, their slabs of animal intestines, their snakes and turtles, crickets, maggots, whatever. I feel like yelling, "I only want mushrooms! Please just let me buy my mushrooms and get the back to the safety of my room!"

Instead, I smile politely. I am an ambassador for America. I don't want the Thais to join the ranks of the other countries holding the US in disdain. I am not rude and cold. I am warm and friendly, all the while seething and sick on the inside, thinking maybe today will be the day the tears come.

The tears are right there on the verge when a misunderstanding over the price of mushrooms and my inability to understand the Thai language has me leaving the market with twice as many mushrooms as I can use, spending twice as much money as I should have. But it's just too frustrating to make it right.

Forlornly, I pack the mushrooms onto my bike and ride home. As I head off onto the main highway, a drunken man is swaying down the road holding several large empty bottles of booze. It's 6:30 in the morning! He's walking through a pack of nine dogs in the middle of the road, shooing them, riling them up. As my bike quickly approaches, he calls out to me. I swerve to avoid the drunk guy, all the while, slowing down and trying to keep my eyes looking in any direction except in the direction of the dogs. I must avoid eye contact with the dogs.

I am lucky enough to escape this time. I fear my luck might be running out though. Just this week I heard a motorcycle rapidly approaching me from behind as I rode on the shoulder of the road. Deja-vu strikes as I remember exactly a year ago the same sound before I was hit by No-Longer-a-Stranger and her little boy. This time the motorcycle sees me just in time and swerves, missing me by inches, crashing himself into a grassy ditch. (He is okay.)

I finally get to my house, usually a refuge of peace and tranquility, the cold air of the AC soothing my hot temper and flaring emotions. But now it just feels empty and lonely. It's a Sunday. I think of things I could do to occupy my time.

Read a book? I don't have any on hand now.

Clean my house? Too hot.

Watch TV? Don't have one.

Call somebody on the phone? Too expensive.

What I really need is to be understood. I need to make contact with people who speak my language and understand my culture.

What I need...is chocolate.

I get back on my bike and ride to the internet shop, stopping for chocolate ice cream along the way. Maybe it was the chocolate ice cream. Maybe it was writing a long cathartic email to friends and family. I think I feel a bit better. I feel good enough to remember that this, too, shall pass.

I change my mind and will not buy airplane tickets home today.

Chapter 39

Skills for Life

I KNEW FINDING MONEY for the life skills camp would be hard. What I hadn't considered, perhaps due to a state of denial, was the difficulty in getting the buy-in from all the other teachers we were relying on to facilitate the camp. I just assumed my status as the farang-in-residence would have the other teachers banging down the doors begging to be a part of my glorious camps. Silly me.

This buy-in is always necessary because, while I can create the curriculum, I desperately needed the teachers to facilitate the sessions and activities. As a teacher myself, I understood why they'd resist. The last thing a teacher wants is an outsider telling them they have to do more work. And to give up a weekend. With no extra pay.

Truth be told, I'd lived in Thailand long enough now to know the teachers would simply be forced to participate. Their boss would tell them they had to do it. They might piss and moan behind the boss's back, but of course they would do it. Still, in my idealism, I wanted them to want to do it. I wanted them to see the benefits of the life skills camp. I wanted intrinsic motivation! The sustainability of the whole project hinged on their buy-in.

My plan was to invite a bunch of other PCVs to my site and conduct a super fun training for the teachers so they would know how to facilitate the camp. So I did. Basically, we just pretended they were the students and went through the activities as if they were the camp participants. Keep in mind, many of the activities and lessons revolved around taboo subjects to Thai teachers. Alcoholism. Gender discrimination. Sex and birth control. This was scary stuff for these teachers. I imagine plenty of teachers in the US would not actually be thrilled to teach about these topics either.

A funny thing happened at the training. Maybe it was the prestige of having all these farangs in town enthusiastically presenting the material. (The farangs say this is awesome, then by golly, this must be awesome). Or maybe it was my own personal charm and magnetism. Maybe it was the element of surprise, as this was no typical "blah blah" lecture session that they are so used to and expected. These were all hands-on activities designed as much for fun as for learning. For whatever reason, the teachers, who I knew were not looking forward to this, actually began to really engage. Their fun-loving natures came out in full swing. They smiled. They laughed. They had fun. We had their buy-in!

After the training, we all packed up along with 46 students from the 6th and 7th grades and camped at a mountainous national park for two and half days as the teachers taught life skills. It was more successful than I dared hope. They rocked the life skills camp! Fully engaged, students had as much fun as the teachers had in their training. Whether or not we met our goals for these students to make better choices in their future is impossible to gauge. However, after the camp, one 7th grade boy approached me. He was a likable trouble-maker whom I knew well from teaching his class. He told me that because of the life skills camp, he didn't want to drink alcohol or smoke cigarettes anymore. He said he hoped for a healthier future. I had to turn away to hide my tears and to keep from embracing him on the spot.

Years later, Somjai would email me letters about life back in my Thai town with news from School 1. She told me the young teachers at School 1 took the reins on this life skills camp and made it their own. These were the middle school teachers, young, vibrant and energetic. She said I would be proud because every year they hold a life skills camp. The camp has come to be seen as so valuable the school actually funds it. The project had become sustainable.

*   *   *

Those teachers actually became role models for me, as I continued my adventures as a Peace Corps volunteer. When I still remained resistant to opportunities because they were challenging to me, I'd think of those teachers. If they could be pushed out of their comfort zone to take on these taboo topics and teach new ideas, surely I could step out of my comfort zone and embrace something difficult. I could at least try something I didn't want to do.

For over a year my neighbor Pi Aw had been offering to give me cooking lessons. I could think of a million ways I'd rather spend my time. This is nothing against Pi Aw. I like her immensely. Quite simply, I don't like to cook. I have never enjoyed it. I would eat at my neighborhood shop every meal if I could. So I always politely declined the offer.

However, after witnessing these teachers take on the life skills camp with such good attitudes, I wanted to be like them. Not to mention, how embarrassing would it be to return back to the US after two years in Thailand and have to tell people I didn't learn how to cook Thai food!

So now, every Sunday I take a pen and paper over to Pi Aw's kitchen and learn to cook my favorite Thai dishes. Other curious neighbors, all women of course, join in. They can't stand to miss an opportunity to socialize and they can't resist witnessing how the farang fares in the Thai kitchen.

Forget the pen and paper. The experience is a delightful party of the senses, the colors of the chilies, vibrantly red or various shades of green. The sounds of "bok bok," as we grind the chilies into a thick paste with a mortar and pestle mixes with the chatter and laughter of the women. There must be a hundred Thai variations of this hot sauce. I love it mixed with grilled tomatoes, onions and garlic, these fragrances assault the sense of smell as the chilies open the sinuses. Thai people eat this condiment with rice and some steamed green vegetables. It can be so hot it feels like your tongue is blistering. I swear it's addictive. Then comes the aroma of lemon grass, ginger, scallions and lime leaves boiling together for the famous *tom yam gung*, or hot and sour shrimp soup.

I don't disappoint the curious onlookers. They are mortified that I carry the chilies in my bare hand. One concerned neighbor makes me drop them and physically holds my hands under cold running water. I don't understand the problem until later that night when I go to take my contacts out. While my hands can tolerate the chili oil on my skin, there are plenty of areas of skin that cannot.

They also don't understand why I go to the trouble to peel the garlic. Thai cooks will simply crush the garlic with a knife and throw the whole thing in, skin and all.

The food isn't just for eating. The same woman who held my hands under the water is sporting a lovely bright yellow paste spread all over her face. She doesn't offer it to me. Therefore, I assume it's worn to whiten the skin.

We joke about opening a Thai restaurant together in the US. At least I think we're joking.

When I look back on my Peace Corps experience years from now, the cooking lessons may just be how I characterize the experience. There's something about sitting in a kitchen with a bunch of women, chopping, slicing, laughing. There's something magical about preparing food together that allows for a kind of bonding between women. We've been doing this forever. Back in the caves around the fire, the porches of Thailand, in kitchens everywhere, I'd like to think that women are still sharing in that journey of the senses. I'm reminded of those early mornings washing clothes by hand with my homestay aunties.

As my journey continues and I try to make sense of it all, I notice a change. I'm not the cynical outsider wallowing through the cultural difficulties. I'm not a whiny farang who hates the heat and the lizards who poop in my house. I'm not the ethno-centric Westerner irritated with the constant barrage of Thai language, cultural inconsistencies and invasive neighbors. I'm a Peace Corps volunteer, I'm embracing the opportunity, and I'm doing some good. It took me a whole damn year, and now I feel like the next year couldn't possibly be enough time to complete the job.

Chapter 40

One Year Later

AFTER COUNTLESS FESTIVALS, CAMPS, AND ADVENTURES, fast-forward one year and it's time to go home. I hate goodbyes. It's just my nature. I am the woman famous in all social circles for her "Irish goodbyes." (An Irish goodbye is leaving a group of people without saying goodbye).

A common dialogue after I leave a party goes something like this:

"Where's Amy?"

"She left."

"She didn't say goodbye."

"She never does."

Therefore, upon leaving Thailand, I would have preferred to slip away in the night and just be gone. But Thai custom requires great ceremony, an elaborate goodbye, the kind with which I'm least comfortable. I take a deep breath and like every other challenge, muscle through it.

The going away party is three parts. The first part is with all the students from my school. The students give speeches and sing songs and perform classical Thai dance. I was a goner, sobbing hysterically, starting from the very first speech. And my crying just went on and on and on for the whole damn ceremony, which lasted about five hours. See why I don't like goodbyes? Every time I'd collect myself, some cute Thai kid would say something sweet and I'd be a goner again. The most moving moment of the day is when every single student, more than 300 in all, gets in a long line, approaches me on his/her knees and bows to me. The kindergarteners put their heads all the way to floor, which shows the utmost respect. The older students put their praying hands and bowed forehead to my knee. Every single kid.

The students are then sent off to class, but all the teachers stay with me for the second part of the going away party. Never mind that every one of those 300-plus students are unsupervised for the next two hours. I had insisted on no gifts and asked only for the white strings.

In Thailand, white strings are commonly seen on people's wrists, tied like a bracelet. Sometimes it's only a few strings. Other times it's many, many strings, creating a thick cotton bracelet. The white thread has been blessed in advance by a monk and is intended to provide protection and good health. When the thread makes a circle around the wrist, the power is stronger because the circle is continuous. Often monks tie the string around peoples' wrists in return for a donation. But anybody can give the white string as a blessing or well wishes. It's believed you should wear the string bracelet for at least three days to get the full merit. I'd been told the longer you can wear the bracelet, the better. Hence, often the bracelets seen being worn in Thailand are no longer white, but a grimy grey, from weeks of wear and tear.

The request for white strings at my going-away-party becomes ceremonial, as each teacher takes a turn approaching me with the white string, holding it between their fingers and rubbing it up and down my wrist while wishing luck, happiness, safe travels, and all sorts of good things.

Lastly the mayor and all the officials and workers from my office, as well as teachers and principals from the other two schools, join us for a meal and karaoke. I had finally pulled myself together when they put me in the front of the room and every single guest stepped forward and presented me with a rose or bouquet of roses, wishing me good luck, safe travels, blessings, happiness. They told me they'd miss me. They said they loved me. I even got a "God bless you" in English! Of course I still couldn't understand much of what was said. I wondered why they kept mentioning Peace Corps. That was my mistranslation. They were actually wishing me peace.

Of course saying goodbye to Somjai is the hardest of all. We are very much like sisters. Perhaps we did indeed know each other in a past life. It's comforting to our broken hearts to think that we have future lifetimes together to look forward to.

Like most Peace Corps volunteers upon finishing their term of service, I am filled with regrets. Why didn't I do more? Why didn't I learn the language better? Why didn't I meet more people? I cringe as I reflect on the many mistakes I made. If only I could do it over again.

On the other hand, look at all that I've learned. Look how I've changed.

One way to sum up how I've personally changed is another list of things I never thought I'd do or say.

- My current favorite song is by a Thai pop band.
- I happily obliged when eight Thai women show up at my house to take a whole role of film with pictures of them and me before I leave. (Remember film?)
- I sometimes chose to hang out under the tree with the neighborhood women in the evening instead of hiding safely in my air conditioned box of a room.
- When given a choice of Thai food or Western fare, I often chose Thai food.

Sometimes I really loved it here…

And one thing I really thought I would never say: "I want to marry this man and have his children."

Yes, I really did think Mustapha was the one. After a year of spending most of my weekends in Bangkok to visit him, I decided I would follow him to the ends of the earth. Only he didn't ask me to. He only said goodbye.

One enters the Peace Corps with such idealism and ambition. You want to make a difference. Did I? I don't know if I did in the "make-the-world-a-better-place" sense. But as far as making a difference, how can we all not make some sort of difference by our mere presence? Hopefully, sometimes for the better.

I had some little triumphs: The woman who hit me on my bicycle, No-Longer-A-Stranger, who found the one and only farang she'd ever met was nice. My neighbor girl, A (small a sound, like in apple), who loved me. Even Principal changing her mind about not attending School 3 Principal's funeral. Or going way back to my homestay during training, my sweet bond with Auntie #2. I now realize she was actually a servant. I am forever grateful for her helping me, especially with laundry. The only words we ever shared were "drunk, not crazy," but I loved her and she loved me. I'm pretty sure I'm the only American she'd ever met.

My list of what I gained from the experience is exponentially larger. These gifts affect me every day of my life in how I see the world, how I connect with people, how I relate to myself. My real sense of accomplishment wouldn't even come to fruition until year later when I received an email from Somjai. The middle school teachers were still conducting a Life Skills Camp every year. It had become sustainable.

What's next? What would you do if you had a few thousand baht in your pocket and the freedom to go anywhere and do anything? I'm going to cross a continent on a train. Riding the Trans-Siberian Express is yet one more thing to check off my bucket list. I'll take the long way to board the train in China, traveling up through Vietnam, spending a few days in

Hanoi. And I've always wanted to go to Greece, so now is as good a time as ever, before I get chained down by a job and daily living again. I'd like to travel even more. Morocco holds a great deal of intrigue and appeal to me these days.

I also fantasize about fulfilling my dream, my lifelong ambition to write a book. Do I dare imagine it? It's so scary to imagine putting myself out there on the page like that.

Who knows what my future holds? I'm exhilarated by the possibilities. In the words of the great 80's band Modern English, "The future's open wide!"

Students bow and say goodbye.

Acknowledgments

I'M HUMBLED TO HAVE THIS OPPORTUNITY to acknowledge many of the people who helped make this book possible. My sister Shannon Moen not only supported me through my Peace Corps experience, but printed out every single email I wrote during those two years in Thailand and compiled them in a binder which made the writing of this book possible. Seriously, I didn't remember half of what I'd written in those emails. (I suppose consuming vast amounts of Thai whiskey didn't help.) Thank you, Nanny!

I was sitting on this dream making no progress whatsoever achieving it, until Stephen Lalonde, my former high school teacher, welcomed me into his writing group. It turned out that was just the incentive I needed, and I can't thank Steve enough. I was lucky to have him as a teacher, and am lucky to have him as a mentor now. Kristi Almeida and Kim Verdone, the other members of our writing group, gave invaluable feedback and insights along the way. Thank you for including me in the group and all your help along the way. Kristi, your help with book cover design proves you are a creative genius. Kim, your unique perspectives and thoughtful evaluations buoyed my writing experience.

My dear friend, Isabelle Capri, your proofreading skills are as fabulous as your friendship. Thank you.

Kay Dixon, you are an inspiration! Thank you for sharing your wisdom and experience as a writer and fellow Returned Peace Corps Volunteer. Know you helped pave the way for me as a writer.

I can't thank Russ Davis at Gray Dog Press enough. Notorious for his support of local writers, his patience, expertise, and willingness to walk me through the publishing process was invaluable to me.

My sister Marcia Matthaei not only came to visit me in Thailand, but also helped immensely with the publishing process. I also thank Marcia for introducing me to *Goddesses in Every Woman* by Jean Shinoda Bolen. She loaned me the book in high school, which led to a writing assignment, which stuck in Stephen "Mr." Lalonde's memory, which led to my joining his writing group, which led to the writing of this book!

My brother Dennis McGarry helped with proofreading and offered advice from afar on washing clothes by hand. My sister Barbara Maruska came to visit me and always enthusiastically supported me. My sister Mary Patterson has always supported me and loved me unconditionally. I am grateful to you all.

Countless other individuals back home supported me through my Peace Corps experience. They are too numerous to name here, but I remember you all and thank you for helping make this book possible. You were the ones on my group email list who took the time to read so many emails, some very long, some full of complaining and foul language. Many of you wrote back encouraging words regarding the quality of my writing or reactions to my stories. Your feedback planted the seeds for this book. Others kept my spirits up with tales from back home. Some sent care packages that made my experience so much better. All of you believed in me. I am so grateful.

My Peace Corps friends, some of whom begged me not to include their names in this book, fed this dream while we were in Thailand. Not only did they get me through our Peace Corps experience, but they also talked and joked about my writing this book one day, and they helped me believe it could happen. Sarah, Carolyn, Shana, Alicia, and Mark, you made my Peace Corps experience rich, fun and joyful. You are forever in my heart. I love you all.

Finally, thanks to my daughter Sophia, my cheerleader, for always believing in me. And last but not least, my husband, Mustapha, for tolerating me, which is more challenging than anyone else will ever know.

About the Author

Amy McGarry lives in Spokane, Washington with her husband, daughter and two cats. She teaches English as a Second Language at Mukogawa Fort Wright Institute, the American branch of Mukogawa Women's University in Japan. *I am Farang* is her first book.